iCONLOGiC™

Version: 111219
Page Count: 264
9781944607517 (Perfect-Bound Print Book)
9781944607524 (Coil-Bound Print Book & PDF)
9781944607531 (eBook)

Adobe Captivate 2019:
Beyond the Essentials (2nd Edition)

"Skills and Drills" Learning

Kevin Siegel

Official
IconLogic Certified Adobe Captivate Developer
courseware

IconLogic Certified
Adobe Captivate
Developer

Get certified from the people who **literally** wrote the book on Adobe Captivate

https://www.iconlogic.com/instructor-led-training/certifications.html

iCONLOGiC

"Skills and Drills" Learning

Contents

NOTES

NOTES

NOTES

Notes

iCONLOGiC
"Skills and Drills" Learning

About This Book

This Section Contains Information About:

The Author

Kevin Siegel is the founder and president of IconLogic, Inc. He has written hundreds of step-by-step computer training books on applications such as *Adobe Captivate, Articulate Storyline, Adobe RoboHelp, Adobe Presenter, Adobe Technical Communication Suite, Adobe Dreamweaver, Adobe InDesign, Microsoft Office, Microsoft PowerPoint, QuarkXPress,* and *TechSmith Camtasia.*

Kevin spent five years in the U.S. Coast Guard as an award-winning photojournalist and has three decades' experience as a print publisher, technical writer, instructional designer, and eLearning developer. He is a certified technical trainer, a veteran classroom instructor, and a frequent speaker at trade shows and conventions. Kevin holds multiple certifications from Adobe and CompTIA. He is also a Certified Online Training Professional (COTP) with the International Council for Certified Online Training Professionals (ICCOTP). You can reach Kevin at **ksiegel@iconlogic.com**.

About IconLogic

Founded in 1992, IconLogic is a training, eLearning development, and publishing company offering services to clients across the globe.

As a training company, IconLogic has directly trained thousands of professionals both onsite and online on dozens of applications. As a publishing company, IconLogic has published hundreds of critically acclaimed books and created technical documents for both print and digital publication. And as a development company, IconLogic has produced content for some of the largest companies in the world, including, but not limited to, ADP, ADT, The World Bank, Heineken, EverFi, Bank of America, Fresenius Kabi, FAA, Wells Fargo, American Express, Microsoft, Department of For-Hire Vehicles, Federal Reserve Bank of Richmond, Coast Guard, Marine Corps, Canadian Blood, Canadian Natural Resources, DC Child and Family Services, and the Department of Defense. You can learn more about IconLogic's varied services at www.iconlogic.com.

Book Conventions

Learners learn best by doing, not just by watching or listening. With that simple concept in mind, IconLogic books are created by trainers and/or authors with years of experience training adult learners. Each IconLogic book contains a minimal amount of text and is loaded with hands-on activities, screen captures, and challenge exercises to reinforce newly acquired skills.

This book has been divided into several modules. Because each module builds on lessons learned in a previous module, it is recommended that you complete each module in succession.

Here is the lesson key:

    ❑ instructions for you to follow look like this (the boxes are also used in bulleted lists)

If you are expected to type anything or if something is important, it is set in bold type like this:

    ❑ type **9** into the text area

If you are expected to press a key on your keyboard, the instruction looks like this:

    ❑ press [**shift**]

If you have any comments or questions about this book or any IconLogic services, please see the last page of this section for IconLogic's contact information.

Confidence Checks

As you move through the lessons in this book, you will come across the little guy at the right. He indicates a Confidence Check. Throughout each module, you are guided through hands-on, step-by-step exercises. But at some point you'll have to fend for yourself. That is where Confidence Checks come in. Please be sure to complete each of the challenges because some exercises build on completed Confidence Checks.

Software and Asset Requirements

To complete the lessons presented in this book, you will need Adobe Captivate **version 2019** for the Mac or PC installed on your computer. Captivate does not come with this book but a free trial version can be downloaded from Adobe.com.

You will need to download this book's project assets (data files) that have been created specifically to support this book and this version of Captivate (See the "Book Data Files" section below).

You'll be hearing audio during some of the lessons, so you'll either need a headset or speakers.

Book Data Files (Captivate Project Assets)

You're probably chomping at the bit, ready to dive into Captivate and learn all of the advanced stuff. Not so fast! Do you have some sample projects? What about graphics? Audio files? No? Don't panic. I've got everything you need—I call them data files—and they can be downloaded from the IconLogic website for free.

Windows users: Work through the following activity.

Mac users: Skip the following activity and go to the Mac activity on page x.

Download the Windows Data Files

1. Download the PC student data files necessary to use this book.

    ❑ use a web browser and go to **http://www.iconlogic.com/pc**

    ❑ click the **Captivate 2019: Beyond The Essentials ZIP file (Version 11.5)** link

    A dialog box may open, asking if you want to **Save** or **Open** (or **Run**) the file. On some computers/browsers, the file downloads to your **Downloads** folder without question.

2. Download/save the zip file to your computer. After the file downloads, close the web browser.

3. Extract (Unzip) the data files.

    ❑ locate the **Captivate2019BeyondData** zip file you just downloaded to your computer

    Note: Downloaded files typically go to the **Downloads** folder on your computer.

    ❑ open the downloaded zipped file and **Extract** the contents

    On most PCs, you can right-click the zipped contents and choose **Extract**; on other PCs the extraction process begins automatically once the zipped file is opened or even during the initial download.

NOTES

☐ save the extracted contents to any location on your computer (the desktop is ideal)

There should now be a folder named **Captivate2019BeyondData** on your computer. As you move through the lessons in this book, you will be working with these files.

4. Skip the next activity and go to page xi.

Download the Mac Data Files

1. Download the Mac student data files necessary to use this book.

   ☐ use a web browser and go to **http://www.iconlogic.com/mac**

   ☐ click the **Captivate 2019: Beyond The Essentials (Version 11.5)** link

   The zipped data files are typically downloaded to the **Downloads** folder on your Mac and are automatically extracted into the folder named **Captivate2019BeyondData**.

2. Move the data files folder to your desktop.

   ☐ drag the **Captivate2019BeyondData** folder from the **Downloads** folder to your desktop

3. You can now close the **Downloads** folder window and your web browser.

   Before starting the lessons in this book, review "How Vendor Software Updates Affect This Book" on page xii.

Captivate's Application Preferences

Adobe Captivate is awesome. But like most computer applications, it can misbehave. I've found that when Captivate gets sluggish on my computer or crashes it's frequently because I've got too many applications running and/or not enough system resources (limited hard disk space and/or memory are the primary culprits). In those instances, closing all nonessential applications solves the problem.

However, there are times when nothing I do seems to help improve Captivate's performance (not even a system reboot). In those rare instances, I've found that resetting all of Captivate's Preferences cures what ails the program.

If you need to reset Captivate's Preferences, you'll appreciate an obscure utility that ships with Captivate that will reset all of the Preferences for you. Prior to beginning the first module in this book, I encourage you to reset your Captivate **Preferences** so that your Captivate settings match those shown in the book.

Reset Captivate's Preferences

1. Ensure that Adobe Captivate isn't running.

2. Reset Captivate's Preferences.

   ❑ navigate to the folder where Captivate is installed on your computer

   Note: On Windows, the default location is typically **C:\Program Files** or **Program Files (x86)\Adobe\Adobe Captivate 2019**. On a Macintosh, the default location is typically **Applications > Adobe Captivate 2019**.

   ❑ open the **utils** folder

   You'll find two files of particular interest within the **utils** folder: **CleanPreferencesWin.bat** and **CleanPreferencesMac**.

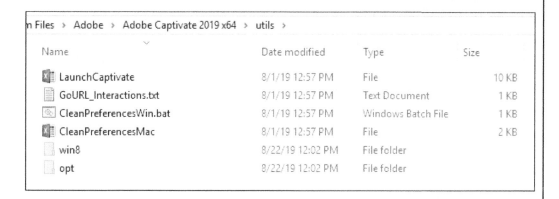

Name	Date modified	Type	Size
LaunchCaptivate	8/1/19 12:57 PM	File	10 KB
GoURL_Interactions.txt	8/1/19 12:57 PM	Text Document	1 KB
CleanPreferencesWin.bat	8/1/19 12:57 PM	Windows Batch File	1 KB
CleanPreferencesMac	8/1/19 12:57 PM	File	2 KB
win8	8/22/19 12:02 PM	File folder	
opt	8/22/19 12:02 PM	File folder	

n Files › Adobe › Adobe Captivate 2019 x64 › utils ›

   ❑ double-click the **CleanPreferences** file appropriate for your operating system

   All of Captivate's application Preferences will be reset to the way they were the first day Captivate was installed on your computer.

NOTES

How Vendor Software Updates Affect This Book

This book was written specifically to teach you how to use Adobe Captivate 2019 Release. The specific version used for the creation of this book was originally **11.1** and this book was updated in October 2019 to fully support the changes introduced by Adobe with version **11.5.1.499**.

With each major release of Captivate, my intention is to write a new book to support that version and make it available within 30-60 days of the software being released by Adobe. From time to time, Adobe makes service releases/patches of Captivate available for customers that fix bugs or add functionality. Usually these updates are minor (bug fixes) and have little or no impact on the lessons presented in this book. However, Adobe sometimes makes significant changes to the way Captivate looks or behaves, even with minor patches. (Such was the case when Adobe updated Captivate from version 5 to 5.5—about a dozen features were added, and a few panels were renamed, throwing readers of those books into a tizzy.)

Because it is not possible for me to recall and update printed books, some instructions you are asked to follow in this book may not match the patched/updated version of Captivate that you are using. If something on your screen does not match what I am showing in the book, please visit the Adobe Captivate 2019 book product page on my website for possible updates (http://www.iconlogic.com/adobe-captivate-2019-beyond-essentials-workbook.html). You can also contact me directly using the information below.

Contacting IconLogic

IconLogic, Inc.
Phone: 410.956.4949, ext. 711
Web: www.iconlogic.com
Email: ksiegel@iconlogic.com

iCONLOGiC

"Skills and Drills" Learning

Rank Your Skills

Before starting this book, complete the skills assessment on the next page.

Skills Assessment

How This Assessment Works

Below you will find 10 course objectives for *Adobe Captivate 2019: Beyond The Essentials (Second Edition)*. **Before starting the book:** Review each objective and rank your skills using the scale next to each objective. A rank of ① means **No Confidence** in the skill. A rank of ⑤ means **Total Confidence**. After you've completed this assessment, go through the entire book. **After finishing the book:** Review each objective and rank your skills now that you've completed the book. Most people see dramatic improvements in the second assessment after completing the lessons in this book.

Before-Class Skills Assessment

1.	I can edit a Text Capture Template.	①	②	③	④	⑤
2.	I can create a responsive project using Fluid Boxes.	①	②	③	④	⑤
3.	I can create a virtual reality project.	①	②	③	④	⑤
4.	I can add interactivity to a video.	①	②	③	④	⑤
5.	I can add accessibility text to slides.	①	②	③	④	⑤
6.	I can create a responsive project using Breakpoints.	①	②	③	④	⑤
7.	I can create a User Variable.	①	②	③	④	⑤
8.	I can create a master slide.	①	②	③	④	⑤
9.	I can create a Conditional Action.	①	②	③	④	⑤
10.	I can create a Manifest file for an LMS.	①	②	③	④	⑤

After-Class Skills Assessment

1.	I can edit a Text Capture Template.	①	②	③	④	⑤
2.	I can create a responsive project using Fluid Boxes.	①	②	③	④	⑤
3.	I can create a virtual reality project.	①	②	③	④	⑤
4.	I can add interactivity to a video.	①	②	③	④	⑤
5.	I can add accessibility text to slides.	①	②	③	④	⑤
6.	I can create a responsive project using Breakpoints.	①	②	③	④	⑤
7.	I can create a User Variable.	①	②	③	④	⑤
8.	I can create a master slide.	①	②	③	④	⑤
9.	I can create a Conditional Action.	①	②	③	④	⑤
10.	I can create a Manifest file for an LMS.	①	②	③	④	⑤

IconLogic, Inc.
"Skills and Drills" Learning
Web: www.iconlogic.com | Email: info@iconlogic.com

iCONLOGiC

"Skills and Drills" Learning

Module 1: Caption Pre-Editing

In This Module You Will Learn About:

- Screen Recording Rehearsals, page 2
- Custom Software Simulations, page 4
- Caption Pre-Editing, page 11

And You Will Learn To:

- Rehearse a Script, page 3
- Set Recording Preferences, page 4
- Record a Simulation, page 7
- Edit a Text Capture Template, page 11

Screen Recording Rehearsals

You have been asked to create an eLearning course that teaches new employees at your company how to use the utilities on the computer such as **Notepad** (Windows) or **TextEdit** (Macintosh). One of the lessons you plan to record using Captivate includes how to change the page orientation within Notepad or TextEdit.

Here is a sample script showing the kind of detailed, step-by-step instructions you need to create or receive from a Subject Matter Expert (SME). You are expected to perform each step written below in either Notepad or TextEdit.

Dear Captivate developer, using either Notepad or TextEdit, record the process of changing the Page Orientation from Portrait to Landscape and then back again (from Landscape to Portrait). Create the recording using a capture size of 1280 x 720. Thanks. Your pal, the Subject Matter Expert.

1. Click the File menu.

2. Click the Page Setup menu item.

3. Click the Landscape orientation button.

4. Click the OK button.

5. Click the File menu.

6. Click the Page Setup menu item.

7. Click the Portrait orientation button.

8. Click the OK button.

9. Stop the recording process.

The script sounds simple. However, you will not know what kind of trouble you might get into unless you rehearse the script prior to recording the process written in the script with Captivate. Let's run a rehearsal, just as if you were a big-time movie director and you were in charge of a blockbuster movie.

Places everyone... and quiet on the set...

Guided Activity 1: Rehearse a Script

1. Start either Notepad (Windows) or TextEdit (Mac).

   The process of starting either Notepad or TextEdit varies slightly, depending on your operating system. For instance, if you are using Windows, use the **Search** feature to start Notepad. If you are using a Mac, choose **Go > Applications**. Locate and open **TextEdit** and create a New document.

   In the images below, Notepad is pictured at the left; TextEdit is at the right.

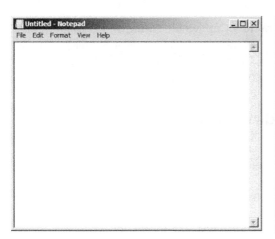 

2. Rehearse the script.

   ☐ using either Notepad or TextEdit (not Captivate), click the **File** menu

   ☐ click the **Page Setup** menu item

   ☐ from the **Orientation** area, click **Landscape**

   Note: In Notepad, Landscape is listed as the word "Landscape." In TextEdit, Landscape is the **second** tool to the right of Orientation (shown below).

   ☐ click the **OK** button

   ☐ click the **File** menu

   ☐ click the **Page Setup** menu item

   ☐ click the **Portrait** orientation button

   ☐ click the **OK** button

   Even though there were no visual changes made to the Notepad document that indicate that the page orientation has changed, the steps you took based on the script worked perfectly (there were no surprises). You will perform these exact steps again in a few moments—for real. As you do, Captivate will record the steps by creating a screen capture each time you click the mouse.

Custom Software Simulations

You can record software demonstrations, simulations, or videos using Adobe Captivate. Typical software demonstrations include text captions that explain what's about to happen and a mouse that moves across the screen to perform the described action. With an assessment simulation you typically include interactive hotspots (click boxes) allowing the learner to perform each step.

Between passive demonstrations and interactive assessment simulations, I recommend simulations because, in my experience, effective eLearning begins and ends with learner engagement. By creating a simulation, the learner performs each step as you're teaching the concept and remains consistently immersed in the lesson—and engaged.

When recording the screen, I recommend you use Captivate's **Custom** recording mode. This mode effectively combines Captivate's Demonstration and Assessment Simulation modes. Using the Custom recording mode when you record, Captivate automatically adds text captions and click boxes throughout the lesson that totally engage your learner.

Guided Activity 2: Set Recording Preferences

1. Ensure that either Notepad or TextEdit is running and start **Adobe Captivate**. (No projects should be open at this point.)

2. Set the Custom Mode Preferences for the simulation you are about to record.

   ☐ Windows users, choose **Edit > Preferences**;
   Mac users, choose **Adobe Captivate > Preferences**

   ☐ from the **Recording** category at the left of the dialog box, click **Modes**

   ☐ from the **Mode** drop-down menu, choose **Custom**

   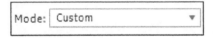

   ☐ from the **Captions** area, select **Add Text Captions**

   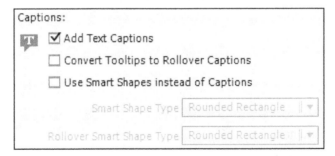

   ☐ from the **Click Boxes** area, select **Add Click Boxes on Mouse Click**

   ☐ from the **Click Boxes** area, select **Failure Caption**

   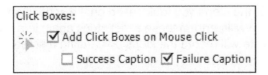

   You selected **Add Text Captions** so that the Text Captions are added for you during the recording phase. *Nice.* And because the captions are written in the imperative, you may be able to use them in the new lesson with little editing. *Nicer.* Everything else has been left deselected except for **Click Boxes** and **Failure Caption**. These two settings result in a highly interactive software simulation out of the box. *Nicest!*

3. Select a caption to use during the recording process.

   ❏ from the **Recording** category at the left of the dialog box, click **Defaults**

   ❏ from the **Text Caption** drop-down menu, ensure **[Default Capture Caption Style]** is selected

   Global Preferences: Recording: Defaults

   Objects:

   Text Caption: | [Default Capture Caption Style] ▼ |

   Each of the text captions that get created during the recording process will use the Default Capture Caption Style. You will soon use the Object Style Manager to control the look of the Default Capture Caption Style.

4. Customize the "To Stop Recording" keyboard shortcut.

   ❏ from the **Recording** category, select **Keys - (Global)**

   ❏ click in the **To Stop Recording** field and press the [**shift**] [**Y**] keys on your keyboard

   To Stop Recording: | Shift+Y |

   If you were to move forward and record a lesson using Captivate, you would press [**shift**] [**Y**] on your keyboard to end the recording process. You can customize the fields in this dialog box to suit your needs. For Windows users, the default key ([**End**]) works great.

5. Reset the default Recording Keys.

   ❏ still in the **Keys - (Global)** area, click the **Restore Defaults** button

   Restore Defaults

   Mac users: On my Mac, the default **To Stop Recording** shortcut keys [**Cmd**] [**Enter**] works on my MacBook Pro only when I'm using an external extended keyboard. When I'm on the road and I don't have that keyboard, I change the keyboard shortcut to [**control**] [**e**] (e for END) and things work perfectly. I would suggest that you experiment and find a keyboard shortcut that works best for you.

   ❏ click the **OK** button

6. Use the Object Style Manager to format the Default Capture Caption Style.

   ❏ choose **Edit > Object Style Manager**

   The Object Style Manager dialog box opens.

   ❏ from the middle of the dialog box, select **[Default Capture Caption Style]**

NOTES

☐ from the **Caption** drop-down menu, choose any **Caption Type** you like

☐ from the **Text Format** area, select any font (**Family**), **Size**, and **Align** you like

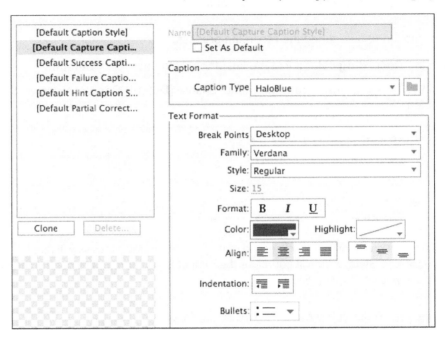

☐ click the **OK** button

Now that you've gotten some settings out of the way, it's time to record the software simulation.

Guided Activity 3: Record a Simulation

1. Determine what Captivate records.

   ☐ on Captivate's Welcome screen, click the **New** tab

   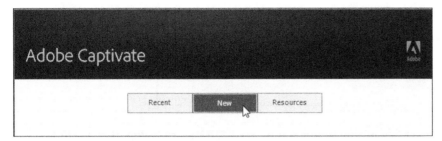

   ☐ double-click **Software Simulation** (or choose **File > Record a New > Software Simulation**)

   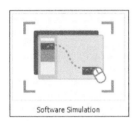

   On your computer display, notice two things besides Notepad or TextEdit. First, there is a large red-bordered box. This is Captivate's **recording area**. Second, there is a control panel containing **Size** and **Recording Type** areas. (Pictured below is a Windows-based desktop that shows Notepad, Captivate's control panel, and the red-bordered recording area.)

   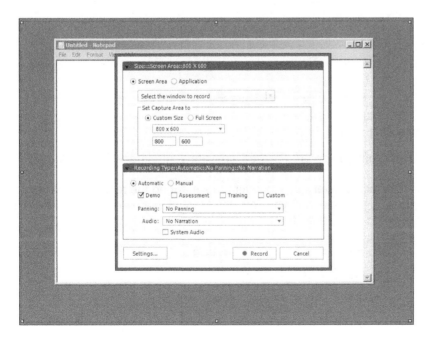

   ☐ from the top left of the Captivate control panel, select **Screen Area**

❏ from the **Set Capture Area to** area of the Control panel, select **Custom Size** and then choose **1280 x 720** from the drop-down menu

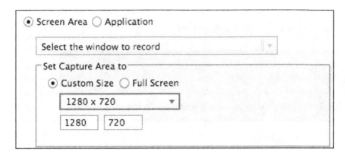

❏ move the Captivate recording area so that it covers Notepad or TextEdit

❏ resize Notepad or TextEdit so that the program window fits nicely within the Captivate recording area (Mac users, consider moving the recording area over the TextEdit menus as shown below. Also, if you want to see the TextEdit ruler shown in the image below, choose **Format > Make Rich Text** from within TextEdit.)

2. Select the recording mode.

❏ from the **Recording Type** area of the Captivate control panel, select **Automatic**

With Automatic selected, every click of your mouse during the recording process creates a screen capture. In contrast, had you selected Manual mode, you would need to use a keyboard shortcut to capture each click you make.

❏ from the **Recording Type** area, select **Custom**

❏ deselect the other modes as necessary

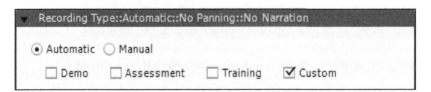

❏ ensure that **Panning** is set to **No Panning** and that **Audio** is set to **No Narration**

Panning:	No Panning	▼
Audio:	No Narration	▼
	☐ System Audio	

Panning is appropriate when you want to record an action outside of the recording area. It's not something you need to use in your upcoming recording. And because there's no voiceover audio needed for this lesson, you've left Audio set to No Narration.

3. Record screen actions.

   ❏ on the Captivate control panel, click the **Record** button

   ❏ once the 3-2-1 countdown goes away, use your mouse to click the **File** menu within Notepad or TextEdit

   If your computer has sound capabilities, you will hear a screen-capture sound every time you click that sounds like the shutter of a camera.

   ❏ click the **Page Setup** menu item

   ❏ from the **Orientation** area, click **Landscape**

   ❏ click the **OK** button

   ❏ click the **File** menu

   ❏ click the **Page Setup** menu item

   ❏ click the **Portrait** orientation button

   ❏ lick the **OK** button

4. Stop the recording process using the **Stop Recording** key (discussed on page 5).

   Note: If the recording doesn't end after pressing your Stop Recording keys, an alternative technique for stopping the recording process is to click the Captivate icon on the System Tray (Windows) or Dock (Mac).

5. Preview the project. (**Preview > Project**)

   As you move through the recording, there are Click Boxes (hot spots) that make this lesson interactive. Also notice that the Text Captions are written in the imperative to encourage learner interactivity. There may be one or two captions you need to edit, and some of the background objects are likely misnamed, especially on the Mac side. Nevertheless, much of the work has been done for you.

Show Properties	⌥⌘P
Page Setup...	⇧⌘P
Print..	

Select the **Page Setup...** menu item

6. When you are finished previewing the project, close the preview and then close the project (there is no need to save it).

NOTES

Custom Recording Confidence Check

You have been asked to bookmark a website so it can be accessed quickly in the future. The process of creating a bookmark (also known as a Favorite) varies depending on the web browser you are using and your operating system. For instance, if you are on a PC and you're using **Microsoft Edge** or **Internet Explorer**, click the **Favorites** icon (which looks like a star) and click **Add**.

If you are using **Google Chrome** or **Firefox**, click the **Bookmark** tool (like Edge and Explorer, the tool looks like a star), and then click the **Done** button.

On **Safari** for the Mac, choose **Bookmarks > Add Bookmark**.

Now that you know how to bookmark a web page, here's your challenge:

1. Use Captivate's **Custom** recording mode to create a software simulation for creating a Bookmark/Favorite for any website that you like (use your favorite browser).

   Forgotten how to record a Custom software simulation? See page 7.

2. When finished recording, save the new project to the **Captivate2019BeyondData** folder as **CreateFavorite**.

3. Preview the project.

   Notice that there are text captions and interactivity, which is wonderful. However, none of the captions contain end-of-sentence punctuation. Although I am not a fan of end-of-sentence punctuation, many corporate style guides insist on end-of-sentence punctuation.

While you could easily add the period at the end of the caption now, it would have been nice if Captivate had put the punctuation in for you when the captions were created. Believe it or not, it is possible to "pre-edit" the text captions and change, among other things, the text that appears in the captions and the way Captivate treats end-of-sentence punctuation. You'll delve into that next. This little bit of wizardry just might save hours of content editing.

Caption Pre-Editing

When you record screen actions, Captivate automatically creates the text captions (provided you ensure **Add Text Captions** is selected via the Mode preferences). The text in those automatic captions is written in the imperative, which is fine. However, there are a couple of ways to write an instruction. For instance, if you want to instruct a learner to *select the New command* from a menu, you could lead the instruction with the word "Select" or "Choose." In effect, the text in the caption could be written two ways: "**Select** the New menu item" or "**Choose** the New menu item."

By default, Captivate uses the word "Select" when it creates the text captions. If you want the captions to instead use the word "Choose," you will have to make the change manually after the recording process is complete. Although not difficult, this kind of editing is labor intensive.

What about end-of-sentence punctuation? For instance, should the captions end with a period or nothing? It's a debatable topic. Do you or don't you? I don't, but you might.

To cut down on text editing in Captivate once the recording process is complete, you can pre-edit the text captions by modifying one of the language template files that are stored in the Captivate application folder on your hard drive. Captivate uses text capture template files to create the text captions.

Guided Activity 4: Edit a Text Capture Template

1. Minimize/Hide Adobe Captivate.

2. Locate the file that controls the text that appears in automatic text captions.

   ❑ using Windows Explorer or Finder, navigate to the folder where **Adobe Captivate 2019** is installed on your computer (Windows users, the path is typically **C:\Program Files** or **Program Files (x86)\Adobe\Adobe Captivate 2019**; Mac users, Captivate is typically in **Applications > Adobe Captivate 2019**.)

   ❑ find (but do not open) **CaptureTextTemplates_English.rdl** file

   This next step is possibly the most important. You are going to create a **copy** of the English RDL file. If you mess up the duplicate RDL file, no worries because you can throw it away. The changes you are about to make to the duplicate RDL file will neither impact the original RDL file nor negatively impact Captivate in any way.

3. Make a copy of the CaptureTextTemplates_English.rdl file.

   ❑ select the **CaptureTextTemplates_English.rdl** file and then **copy** and **paste** it into the Captivate application folder (the current folder)

   Note: You may be prompted to confirm the action, which you should do. Because you are pasting a file directly within the application folder, you may be blocked completely because of limited read/write access to the application folder. In that case, you may need someone from your IT team to grant you read/write access to the Captivate application folder on your computer.

   You might also be able to first save the file to your **Desktop**, make the upcoming edits, and then copy/paste the RDL file into the application folder. If you are unable to make changes to the RDL file and get it into the Adobe Captivate 2019 application folder, you will not be unable to complete the remaining steps in this module.

NOTES

4. Rename the duplicate RDL file.

☐ change the name of the duplicate RDL file to
CaptureTextTemplates_YourFirstName.rdl

Check for typos in your new file name. In the image below, notice that Biff has created an RDL file named **CaptureTextTemplates_Biff.rdl**. You will be editing your personal RDL file next.

5. Open CaptureTextTemplates_YourFirstName.rdl with **NotePad** (Windows) or **TextEdit** (Mac).

☐ double-click your **RDL** file

If the file does not automatically open within NotePad (Windows) or TextEdit (Mac), you will need to lend a helping hand.

Windows users, a "File Association Helper" dialog box (or similar) will open. Choose **Search through windows** or **Select a program from a list of installed programs** and then click the **Search** or **OK** button. (You might also see a message that says "How do you want to open this file?" If so, click "More apps.")

Mac users, select **Choose Application**

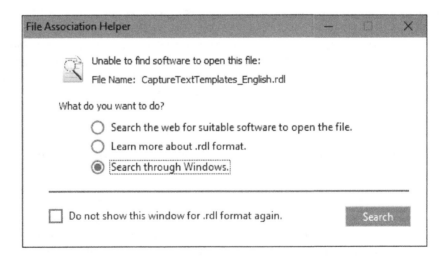

The **Open With** dialog box (Windows) or **Choose Application** dialog box (Mac) appears.

☐ Windows users, select **Notepad** from the list of available programs and click **OK**;
Mac users, select **TextEdit**

In the images below, the Windows 10 options are shown first; the Macintosh **Choose Application** dialog box is shown second.

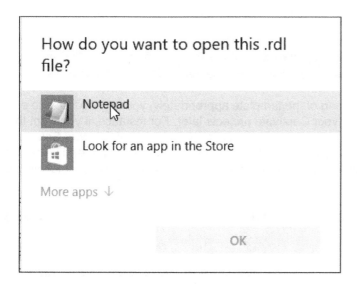

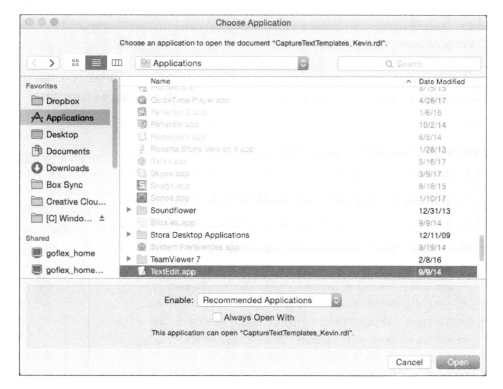

The RDL file opens in the text editor. If you are familiar with programming languages like HTML or XML, you will likely recognize the tags used in the document. If you do not have programming experience, no worries, you will be able to edit the template either way.

6. Edit the RDL file.

❑ scroll down to the part of the document shown below (if you have trouble finding the text, use the Find feature available in both Notepad and TextEdit to find **Object Name="Menu"**)

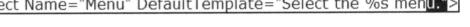

```
<Object Name="Menu" DefaultTemplate="Select the %s menu">
```

If you edit the text in this part of the template appropriately, you might be able to eliminate some text editing in all of your Captivate projects later. For instance, if you want the word **Choose** to always appear in Captivate's text captions instead of the word **Select**, you'd change the word **Select** to **Choose** in the template prior to recording. And if you want the text captions to end with a period, all you'd need to do is add a period to the left of the closing quote.

❑ at the end of the **Object Name="Menu"** line, click between the **u** in the word **menu** and the **closing quote**

❑ type a period (.)

```
<Object Name="Menu" DefaultTemplate="Select the %s menu.">
```

7. Save your work. (Keep the file open.)

Note: If you experience trouble saving the RDL file to your hard drive, you may succeed by first saving the RDL to the desktop. From there, you can copy/paste the RDL file into the Adobe Captivate folder.

RDL Editing Confidence Check

1. In the image below, notice that I've added periods to the end of several lines of text. Spend a few moments adding periods on your own.

```
<Object Name="Menu" DefaultTemplate="Select the %s menu.">
    <Event Name="LeftDBClick" Template="Double-click the %s menu."/>
    <Event Name="RightClick" Template="Right Click the %s menu."/>
    <Event Name="RightDBClick" Template="Double-click the %s menu."/>
    <Event Name="MiddleDBClick" Template="Double-click the %s menu."/>
    <Event Name="KeyPress" Template="Press %s key for %s menu."/>
</Object>
<Object Name="MenuItem" DefaultTemplate="Select the %s menu item.">
    <Event Name="LeftDBClick" Template="Double-click the %s menu item."/>
    <Event Name="RightClick" Template="Right Click the %s menu item."/>
    <Event Name="RightDBClick" Template="Double-click the %s menu item."/>
    <Event Name="MiddleDBClick" Template="Double-click the %s menu item."/>
    <Event Name="KeyPress" Template="Press %s key for %s menu item."/>
```

2. As an experiment, change the words **Select the %s menu item** to **Choose the %s command**. (During the recording process, let's see if this has any effect on the text that appears in the text captions.)

3. Save and close the text file.

   Note: If you had to work on the text file via your desktop, remember to **copy** the file and **paste** it into the Captivate application folder. If the edited RDL file isn't located within the Captivate application folder, your RDL file will not appear in the **Generate Captions In** drop-down menu as shown below.

4. Return to Captivate and open Captivate's **Preferences** dialog box.

5. Select the **Recording** category from the list at the left.

6. Select your name from the **Generate Captions In** drop-down menu.

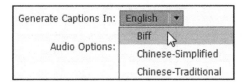

7. Using your browser of choice, use the **Custom** recording mode to create another simulation that covers the process of creating a Bookmark (Favorite) to any website you like. During the recording process, also select a menu or two and a menu item.

   Need help recording screen actions using Custom mode? See page 4.

8. When finished recording, save the new project to the **Captivate2019BeyondData** folder as **CreateFavorite_CustomCaptions**.

9. Preview the project.

   The text captions should now contain end-of-sentence punctuation. In addition, if you used a menu when creating the Favorite, the text in the captions where you selected a menu command should now begin with **Choose** instead of **Select** and end with **command** instead of **menu item**.

10. Close the preview.

11. Save and close all open projects.

    Notes: Changes made to an RDL file will have no effect on existing Captivate projects. Only new recordings that specifically use your RDL file will be affected. And you can elect to go back and use the original English RDL file at any time. Prior to recording new screen actions, display the **Preferences** dialog box, **Recording** category. Choose **English** from the **Generate Captions In** drop-down menu.

Notes

iCONLOGiC

"Skills and Drills" Learning

Module 2: Object Styles, Project Sharing, and Branching

In This Module You Will Learn About:

And You Will Learn To:

Object Styles

It might be an understatement, but consistency among slides in a project (and from project to project) is important. Few things lower the professional look and feel of a project or course than dissimilar slide objects, such as the haphazard use of fonts, sizes, and colors. Fortunately, you can elect to apply Object Styles that ship with Captivate to just about any slide object. Object Styles contain myriad formatting options designed to ensure that slide objects are formatted consistently. If you need to follow your own corporate standards and style guide, you can create your own custom Object Styles.

Guided Activity 5: Create a New Style

1. Open **RenameFolder** from the Captivate2019BeyondData folder.

2. If you see the **Update Missing Fonts** dialog box, click **Don't show this dialog box on opening this project**, and then click the **Close** button.

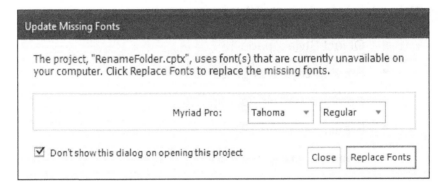

The **Update Missing Fonts** dialog box started appearing in Captivate 11.5 and is useful if you no longer have a project's fonts on your computer. Perhaps a colleague used proprietary fonts, you've inherited the project, and you do not have access to the same fonts. Although all of the projects used in this book were created in older versions of Captivate and then upgraded to Captivate 11.5, the only fonts used throughout are Verdana (which is definitely on your computer) or other standard fonts. For all projects referenced in this book, clicking the **Close** button is appropriate whenever you come across the Update Missing Fonts dialog box.

When it comes to font selections, we tend to stick with Verdana for most of our eLearning development. Why? Verdana is easy to read onscreen. In addition, it's a web safe font, meaning most computers, devices, and operating systems support Verdana and the font will look pretty much the same on most devices. However, many designers go with alternative fonts. If you use alternative fonts in your projects, learners who don't have that font will see a replacement font selected by their web browser.

Adobe Captivate includes access to **Adobe Fonts**. When Adobe Fonts are used in your projects, learners always see the correct fonts when they access your eLearning content. To access Adobe Fonts, select a caption in your project and then look for the Adobe Fonts icon (shown highlighted below) via the **Properties Inspector > Style > Character**.

Although Adobe Fonts integration is not covered in this book, there is a helpful video created by fellow Captivate developer **Paul Wilson** that demonstrates the Adobe Fonts process via this URL: **https://adobe.ly/2sAWRNc**.

3. Preview the project.

   As you watch the preview, pay particular attention to the appearance of the project's text captions. The Caption Type is **HaloRed**, and the font is Times New Roman. Simply put, this project's formatting needs some work.

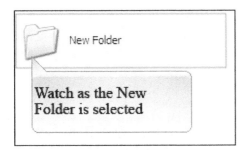

4. Close the preview.

5. Close the project (do not save the project if prompted).

6. Open **FeedMe** from the Captivate2019BeyondData folder.

7. Save the project to the Captivate2019BeyondData folder as **CreatingRenamingFolders**.

8. Preview the project.

   This nine-slide project contains text captions that already look much better than those in the RenameFolder project. You are going to make some slight changes to one of the text captions and save those changes as a new style.

9. Close the preview.

10. Reset an Object Style.

    ☐ go to slide **8**

    ☐ select the text caption "Watch as the new Folder is selected"

    Observe the **Style Name** area of the **Properties Inspector**. The selected caption is using the **Default Caption Style**. However, at some point it was manually formatted using options on the Properties Inspector. You can tell that an object was manually formatted by the **plus sign** that appears to the left of the style's name in the Style Name drop-down menu.

Although there is nothing wrong with manually formatting slide objects, using Object Styles speeds up your work and is helpful in ensuring that objects in a project are consistently formatted.

❑ on the **Properties Inspector**, click the menu  to the right of **Style Name**

❑ choose **Reset Style**

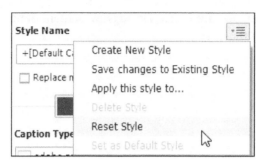

Selecting Reset Style removes all of the manual formatting applied to the selected caption. The caption should now look like the other text captions in the project.

11. Change the properties of a text caption.

❑ go to another slide and select any text caption

On the Properties Inspector, notice that the selected text caption is using the Default Caption Style. There's no plus sign, so the object is using the Object Style without any overrides.

❑ on the Properties Inspector, select the **Style** tab

❑ from the **Caption Type** drop-down menu, choose **Frosted**

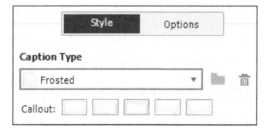

❑ from the **Character** area, change the Font Size to **14**

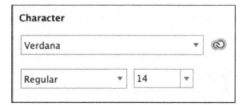

On the Properties Inspector, notice that the Default Caption Style has a plus sign to the left of the style name. The plus sign is an indication of a style override.

12. Create a new style.

☐ on the **Properties Inspector**, click the menu to the right of **Style Name** and choose **Create New Style**

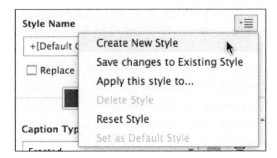

The Save New Object Style dialog box opens.

☐ name the new Object Style: **SSS_TextCaptions**

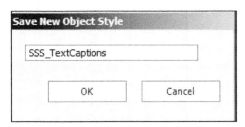

☐ click the **OK** button

The new style is immediately applied to the text caption you modified. In addition, the style appears in the Style drop-down menu on the Properties Inspector.

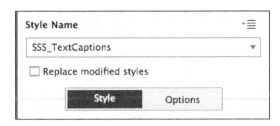

13. Save your work.

Guided Activity 6: Apply an Object Style Globally

1. Ensure that the **CreatingRenamingFolders** project is still open.

2. Apply a text caption style to all of the project's text captions at one time.

   ☐ ensure that the text caption you formatted during the last activity is selected

   ☐ on the **Properties Inspector**, click the menu to the right of **Style Name** and choose **Apply this style to**

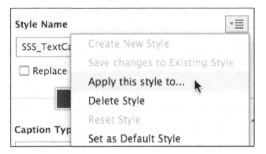

The Apply Object Style dialog box opens.

   ☐ ensure that **Default Caption Style** appears in the drop-down menu

   ☐ click the **OK** button

Because all of the text captions in the project are using the Default Caption Style (except the one caption that you reformatted), every text caption in the project is now using the new SSS_TextCaptions style.

3. Save your work.

Sharing Styles

When you edit or create Object Styles within one Captivate project, those changes do not appear in other projects. If you would like to share Object Styles with other Captivate developers or use Object Styles created by another developer in your project, Captivate's ability to both import and export styles will prove useful. The export files have a **CPS** extension and can be imported only into Captivate.

Guided Activity 7: Export and Import an Object Style

1. Ensure that the **CreatingRenamingFolders** project is still open.

2. Export a style.

   ☐ choose **Edit > Object Style Manager**

   The Object Style Manager dialog box opens.

   ☐ from the top center of the dialog box, select the **SSS_TextCaptions** style you created earlier

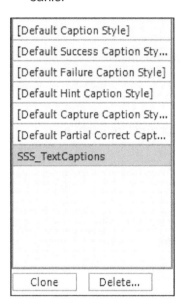

   ☐ from the bottom of the dialog box, click the drop-down menu between the **Import** and **Export** buttons

   ☐ if necessary, select **Selected style only**

   ☐ click the **Export** button

   ☐ confirm that the name of the file to be exported is **SSS_TextCaptions.cps**

   ☐ save the file to the **Captivate2019BeyondData** folder

❑ click the **OK** button to acknowledge the successful export

❑ click the **OK** button to close the Object Style Manager dialog box

3. Save your work (leave the CreatingRenamingFolders project open).

4. Reopen the **RenameFolder** project from the Captivate2019BeyondData folder.

5. Go to slide **2** and notice once again that the caption style and font used does not match the CreatingRenamingFolders project.

6. Import an Object Style.

❑ choose **Edit > Object Style Manager**

❑ from the bottom of the dialog box, click the **Import** button

❑ open the **SSS_TextCaptions.cps** file that you exported a moment ago

You will be asked if you want to overwrite existing styles.

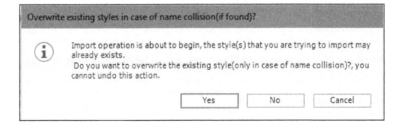

❑ click the **Yes** button

❑ click the **OK** button to acknowledge the successful import

The imported style appears in the list in the middle of the dialog box. You will use the imported style during the Confidence Check that follows.

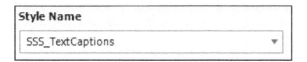

☐ click the **OK** button to close the Object Style Manager dialog box

Styles Confidence Check

1. Still working in the **RenameFolder** project, select the text caption on slide 2.

2. Use the Properties Inspector to apply the imported **SSS_TextCaptions** style to the caption.

Style Name

SSS_TextCaptions   ▼

3. Use the **Apply this style to** command to apply the **SSS_TextCaptions** to all of the project's text captions that are using the Default Caption Style. (You learned how to do this on page 22.)

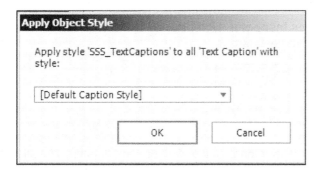

Apply Object Style

Apply style 'SSS_TextCaptions' to all 'Text Caption' with style:

[Default Caption Style]   ▼

OK   Cancel

4. Save your work. (Keep the project open.)

Combining Projects

The recommended play time for published Captivate projects is approximately five minutes. A lesson that plays much longer runs the risk of losing the learner, thanks to any number of distractions prevalent in today's hectic world. On the other hand, shorter playtimes are not necessarily better. If the lesson doesn't contain enough "meat," you will likely find that your learners resent that you had them go to the trouble of starting the lesson in the first place. If the lesson doesn't contain enough content to engage the learner for at least a few minutes, you should consider either not including the lesson in the course or combining the lesson with another lesson. The two projects that you have been playing with over the past few activities (CreatingRenamingFolders and RenameFolder) are both very short. In the next activity, you'll combine them.

Guided Activity 8: Name a Slide

1. Ensure that both the **CreatingRenamingFolders** and **RenameFolder** projects are open.

2. Switch to the **CreatingRenamingFolders** project. (You can click the project's tab to make it the active project.)

3. Name a slide.

   ☐ on the Filmstrip, select slide **1**

   ☐ from the top of the **Properties Inspector**, type **Lesson 1: Create New Folder** into the field and press [**enter**] on your keyboard

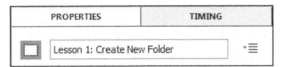

The new name appears below the thumbnail of the slide on the Filmstrip. The slide name proves useful when you are pasting content from one project into another and when you are creating a branching scenario. You will perform both tasks shortly.

4. Save your work.

Naming Confidence Check

1. Name the last slide in the **CreatingRenamingFolders** project **End Lesson 1**.

2. Switch to the **RenameFolder** project and name the first slide **Lesson 2: Renaming Folders**.

3. Name the next to last slide **End Lesson 2** and the last slide **Congrats**.

4. Open the **TOCSlide** project from the Captivate2019BeyondData folder and name the one slide in the project **Home**.

5. Save all three of the open projects. (You can save multiple files at one time by choosing **File > Save All**.)

Guided Activity 9: Copy and Paste Project Assets

1. Ensure that the **CreatingRenamingFolders**, **RenameFolder**, and **TOCSlide** projects are all still open.

2. Copy slides and objects from the RenameFolder project to the clipboard.

   ☐ switch to the **RenameFolder** project and on the Filmstrip, select slide **1**

   ☐ scroll down to the bottom of the Filmstrip, press **[Shift]** on your keyboard, and then select the last slide (Slide 9, the Congrats slide)

   ☐ release the **[Shift]** key

   ☐ choose **Edit > Copy** to copy the selected slides to the clipboard

3. Paste the slides from the clipboard into the another project.

   ☐ switch to the **CreatingRenamingFolders** project

   ☐ scroll down the Filmstrip and select the **last slide** (the End Lesson 1 slide)

   ☐ choose **Edit > Paste**

   And just like that, the assets from the RenameFolder project have been added to the CreatingRenamingFolders project (slides, slide objects, slide names, etc.). The CreatingRenamingFolders project now consists of 18 slides.

4. Copy and paste the assets from the TOCSlide project into the **CreatingRenamingFolders** project.

   ☐ switch to the **TOCSlide** project

   ☐ choose **Edit > Copy** to copy the project's one slide to the clipboard

   ☐ switch to the **CreatingRenamingFolders** project, select the **first slide** in the project, and then choose **Edit > Paste**

   The newly pasted **Home** slide is the second slide on the Filmstrip.

   ☐ on the Filmstrip, drag the **Home** slide into the first position

5. Save and close all of the projects.

Branching

The **CreatingRenamingFolders** project you worked with during the past few activities contains two distinct lessons: **Creating New Folders** and **Renaming Folders**. You combined the two lessons into one course when you copied the assets from the RenameFolder project into the CreatingRenamingFolders project. The first slide in the project is a menu that gives learners access to either section. When you allow learners to choose multiple paths in a lesson, you've created a branch. Because you can have multiple branches in a project, you will appreciate Captivate's Navigation workspace, which provides an overview of where the branches go and what the learner needs to click to follow the branch.

Guided Activity 10: Use Buttons to Create a Branch

1. Open the **BranchMe** project from the Captivate2019BeyondData folder.

   This project is identical to the completed CreatingRenamingFolders project you were working with during the last activity.

   On slide **1** (the Home slide) notice that there are two buttons on the slide, one for each part of the lesson (Create New Folders and Rename Folders).

2. Set the action for a button to jump to a specific slide in the project.

   ☐ on slide **1**, double-click the **Create New Folders** button to open the Properties Inspector

   Note: If you see only the Timing Inspector at the right of the Captivate window (instead of both Properties and Timing), close and then reopen the Properties Inspector.

   ☐ on the Properties Inspector, select the **Actions** tab

   ☐ from the **On Success** drop-down menu, choose **Jump to slide**

   ☐ from the **Slide** drop-down menu, ensure **2 Lesson 1: Create New Folder** is selected

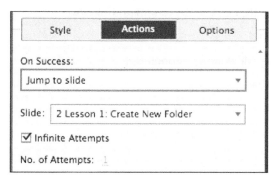

Branching Confidence Check

1. Still working within the **BranchMe** project, set the button Action for the **Rename Folders** button so that it jumps to slide **11, Lesson 2: Renaming Folders**.

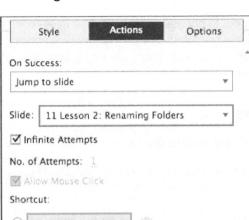

2. Save your work and preview the project.

3. Click the buttons and ensure that their Actions work as expected (the buttons should branch you to either slide **2** or **11**).

4. Close the Preview.

5. On slide **2**, set the properties for the three buttons as follows:

   ☐ **Play Lesson:** Go to the next slide

   ☐ **Home:** Jumps to slide **1** (Home)

   ☐ **Next Lesson:** Jumps to slide **11**, Lesson 2: Renaming Folders

6. On slide **11**, set the properties for the three buttons as follows:

   ☐ **Play Lesson:** Go to the next slide

   ☐ **Home:** Jumps to slide **1** (Home)

   ☐ **Previous Lesson:** Jumps to slide **2**, Lesson 1: Create New Folder

7. On the last slide, set the properties for the two buttons as follows:

   ☐ **Create New Folders:** Jumps to slide **2**, Lesson 1: Create New Folder

   ☐ **Rename Folders:** Jumps to slide **11**, Lesson 2: Renaming Folders

8. Save your work and preview the project.

9. Click the buttons and ensure that they all work as expected.

10. Close the Preview.

11. Close the Project.

Guided Activity 11: Explore the Branching View

1. Open the **NavigateMe** project from the Captivate2019BeyondData folder.

   This project is the same as the BranchMe project except the branches (slide jumps) have been added for you.

2. View the Branching window.

   ☐ choose **Window > Branching View**

   The Branching window opens. By default, the window is split into two main sections. At the top you see the individual branches you set up when you created slide jumps for several buttons throughout the project. The bottom panel contains an orange box that makes it convenient to scroll through long branches.

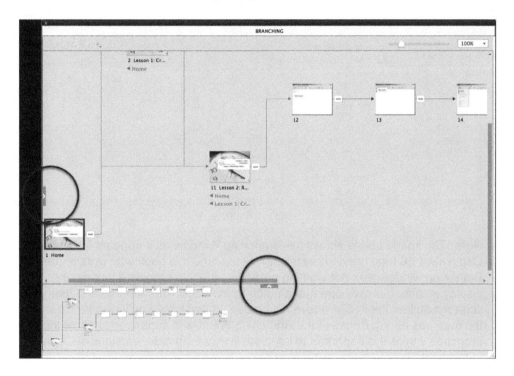

   Notice the two collapse/expand icons, one at the far left and another at the bottom center (shown circled in the image above).

   ☐ click the collapse/expand icon at the **left** of the Branching window

   A third panel opens. This is where you would see stray slides (slides without links). There's also a Legend. The color of the arrows you might see in the main Navigation panel are explained in the Legend.

   ☐ click the collapse/expand icon at the **bottom** of the Branching window

   You either expand or collapse a panel containing the orange box. If you'd like, drag the orange box and notice that doing so allows you to scroll through the branching view.

3. Click both collapse/expand icons as necessary to collapse both the panel at the left and the panel at the bottom.

NOTES

4. Zoom away from the Navigation panel.

   ☐ from the top right of the Branching window, change the magnification to **Best Fit**

You should now be able to clearly see the branches you created during the previous activities. (You can further resize the Branching window by dragging the lower right corner of the window. And you can zoom closer by dragging the zoom slider at the top right of the Branching window.)

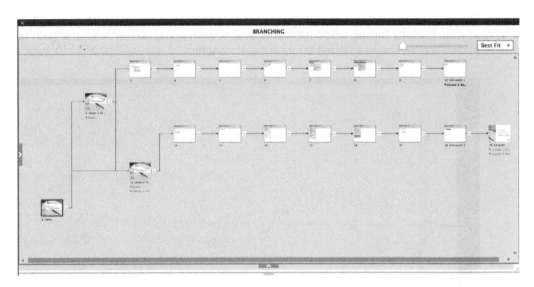

Note: The image above shows the Branching Window as it appears in Adobe Captivate 11.0 (and previous versions). At the time this book was written, the Branching window was not working properly... the two branches incorrectly display as one. It is my hope that a patch from Adobe fixes the bug and that your screen matches the image above. Of course, in that case you'll wonder what all the fuss was about. Because the Branching Window is supposed to show the branches, I think it is important to keep the image from older versions of Captivate in this book.

5. Export the Branching view as an image.

   ☐ at the top left of the Branching window, click the **Export Branching View** tool

The Export branching view dialog box appears.

   ☐ open the **Captivate2019BeyondData** folder

   ☐ save the image as **CreateRename_BranchingView**

❏ select **Jpeg Files** from the **Save as type** area (Windows) or the **File Format** area (Mac)

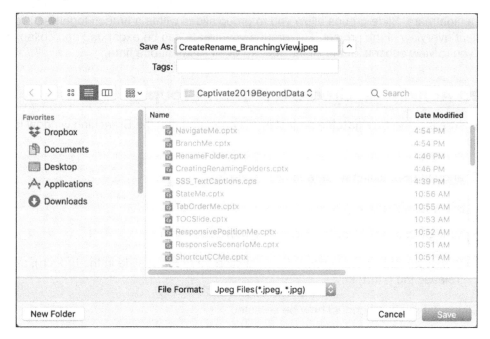

❏ click the **Save** button

❏ click the **OK** button

The image has been exported to the Captivate2019BeyondData folder. You could import the image into any program that accepts images. Or you could email the image to a team member or manager for review.

Branch Groups

If your project is large and contains multiple branches, keeping track of the branches could become a nightmare. Slide groups allow you to group slides within a branch together, providing an excellent overview of the project. The groups you create can be expanded and collapsed, allowing you to view subsets of the slides instead of all slides at one time.

Guided Activity 12: Create a Branch Group

1. Ensure that the **NavigateMe** project is still open and that the Branching window is still open.

2. Change the Branching window view to **Best Fit**.

3. Select a group of slides.

   ☐ in the Branching window, select slide **2 (Lesson 1...)**

   ☐ press [**shift**] on your keyboard, select slide **10** (the last slide in the branch), and then release the [**shift**] key

   Slides **2** through **10** should now be selected.

4. Create a Slide Group.

   ☐ on the Branching window, click the **Create Slide Group** tool

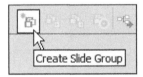

The selected slides are grouped together (shown in the circle below) and no longer take up the horizontal space they once did. By default, the name of the group is **Untitled Group**.

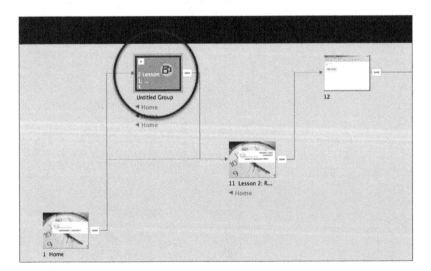

5. Title the new Slide Group.

   ❏ on the Properties Inspector, change the **Title** of the Group to **CreateNewFolder**

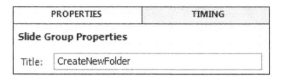

6. View expanding thumbnails of the new Slide Group.

   ❏ point to the middle of the slide group you just created

   The slides in the group open horizontally across the Branching window. When you move your mouse away from the group, the group collapses, once again saving horizontal space on the Branch panel.

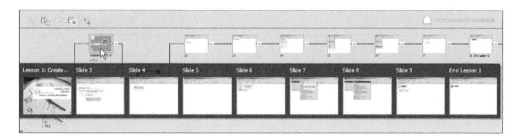

7. Explore the group on the Filmstrip.

   ❏ close the Branching window

   On the Filmstrip, notice that several slides appear to be missing.

   ❏ click the arrow at the upper left of the CreateNewFolder thumbnail

   The group expands revealing all of the slides in the group. You can click the arrow again to collapse the group.

8. Save and close the project.

Notes

iCONLOGiC
"Skills and Drills" Learning

Module 3: Variables and Widgets

In This Module You Will Learn About:

And You Will Learn To:

Variables

Variables serve as placeholders for data. The data can be used to provide feedback to the learner, create Advanced Actions (you will learn to work with Advanced Actions on page 128), add content, or configure widgets (you will learn to work with widgets on page 48).

There are two types of variables available in Adobe Captivate: **System** and **User**. System variables are available in all Captivate projects. These types of variables include **Movie Information** (such as the current slide and frame), **Movie Metadata** (information about the project, such as its name, author, and company), **System Information** (data that can be grabbed from your computer, such as current date and time), and **Quizzing** (lists that allow you to capture quiz data, such as the number of quiz attempts or the percentage of questions answered correctly). **User** variables are created by the developer (you) on an as-needed basis (although all projects include a few User variables by default).

During the next few activities, you'll fill in some project information and see how system variables allow you to display that information within text captions.

Guided Activity 13: Add Project Information

1. Open **VariableWidgetMe** from the Captivate2019BeyondData folder.

2. Add information to the document.

   ☐ choose **File > Project Info**

   The Project Information dialog box opens.

   ☐ in the **Author** field, type **Biff Bifferson**

   ☐ in the **Company** field, type **Super Simplistic Solutions**

   ☐ in the **E-mail** field, type **biff.bifferson@supersimplisticsolutions.com**

   ☐ in the **Website** field, type **www.supersimplisticsolutions.com**

   ☐ in the **Copyright** field, type **Super Simplistic Solutions. All rights reserved.**

   ☐ in the **Project Name** field, type **Working with Variables and Widgets**

   ☐ in the **Description** field, type **This lesson will help you learn how to add variables and widgets to a Captivate project.**

Author:	Biff Bifferson
Company:	Super Simplistic Solutions
E-mail:	biff.bifferson@supersimplisticsolutions.com
Website:	www.supersimplisticsolutions.com
Copyright:	Super Simplistic Solutions. All rights reserved.
Project Name:	Working with Variables and Widgets
Description:	This lesson will help you learn how to add variables and widgets to a Captivate project.

   ☐ click the **OK** button

Guided Activity 14: Insert a System Variable

1. Ensure that the **VariableWidgetMe** project is still open.

2. Insert a text caption.

   ☐ go to slide **1** and choose **Text > Text Caption**

   ☐ type **Welcome to** followed by [**spacebar**]

3. Insert a system variable into the text caption.

   ☐ ensure your insertion point is blinking within the text caption (you cannot insert a variable in a caption without the insertion point)

   ☐ on the **Properties Inspector**, **Character** area, click **Insert Variable**

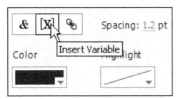

The Insert Variable dialog box opens.

   ☐ from the **Variable Type** drop-down menu, choose **System**

   ☐ from the **View By** drop-down menu, choose **Movie Metadata**

The Movie Metadata is a group of System variables that specifically look into the Project Information dialog box that you just filled out.

   ☐ from the **Variables** drop-down menu, choose **cpInfoProjectName**

   ☐ change the Maximum length to **15**

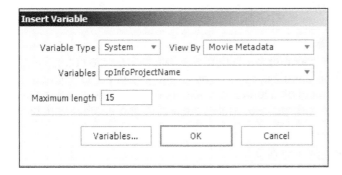

   ☐ click the **OK** button

The variable appears within the text caption.

Variable Preview Confidence Check

1. Drag the text caption and resize it until its size and position look similar to the picture below

2. Save your work.

3. Preview the project.

   Notice two things as the first slide appears. First, the variable gibberish you saw prior to previewing the project has been replaced by the data you typed in the Project Name field back on page 38. *That's cool!* However, the entire name of the project, "Working with Variables and Widgets," isn't showing up.

   > Welcome to Working with Va

   A moment ago you changed the number of characters allowed by the cpInfoProjectName variable to 15 characters (the default is 50). Because the project name is longer than 15 characters, the text has been cut off. During the next activity, you will increase the number of characters allowed by the variable and, while you're at it, add another variable to the text caption.

4. Close the preview (keep the project open).

Guided Activity 15: Edit a System Variable

1. Ensure that the **VariableWidgetMe** project is still open.

2. Edit the maximum number of characters displayed by a variable.

   ☐ on slide **1**, select and delete the variable text **$$cpInfoProjectName$$** from the Text Caption

   ☐ on the **Properties Inspector**, **Character** area, click **Insert Variable**

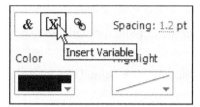

The Insert Variable dialog box reopens.

   ☐ from the **Variable Type** drop-down menu, select **System**

   ☐ from the **View By** drop-down menu, select **Movie Metadata**

   ☐ from the **Variables** drop-down menu, select **cpInfoProjectName**

   ☐ change the **Maximum length** to **25**

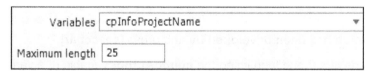

   ☐ click the **OK** button

Before previewing the project and seeing if the Maximum length field has changed things for the better, notice that the text caption resized after you inserted the updated variable. To prevent objects from resizing after you make edits, display the **Preferences** dialog box (PC users: **Edit > Preferences**; Mac users: **Adobe Captivate > Preferences**, from the list at the left, select the first **Defaults**, then deselect **Autosize Captions**.

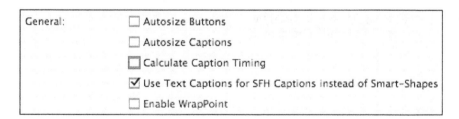

Note: I never allow Captivate to Autosize anything or to calculate the timing for my captions. I find that all three options make more work for me in the long run. For instance, let's say that I leave the first three options shown in the image above selected. I then spend time sizing a caption to a specific size and setting a specific play time for the caption. If I later make even a simple change to the text within the caption (change the font size, for instance, or spell check), both the caption's size *and* timing are reset by Captivate. *More work for me? No thanks!*

NOTES

System Variables Confidence Check

1. Resize the text caption larger (it needs to be big enough to display a few sentences).

2. Preview the project.

   Increasing the maximum length has improved things, to a point. However, the entire project name still doesn't appear. You'll have to make another change to the Maximum length field of the variable.

3. Close the preview and save your work.

4. Still working on slide **1** of the VariableWidgetMe project, delete the variable text **$$cpInfoProjectName$$** in the text caption.

5. Insert the **cpInfoProjectName** variable again. (Notice that the default Maximum length for a Variable is **50**.)

Maximum length | 50

6. Preview the project and confirm that the entire project name appears in the text caption.

7. Close the preview and then save your work.

8. Double-click the text caption on slide **1**, click after the **$$cpInfoProjectName$$**, and type a period to complete the sentence.

9. Press [**enter**] a few times to add some white space.

10. Type **This presentation has been developed by** and press [**spacebar**].

11. Resize the text caption larger and then insert the **cpInfoAuthor** variable (the variable is grouped with the Movie Metadata variables) with a Maximum length of **50**.

12. Press [**spacebar**] after the **$$cpInfoAuthor$$** text and type **of**.

13. Insert the **cpInfoCompany** variable with a Maximum length of **50**.

14. Type a period at the end of the text.

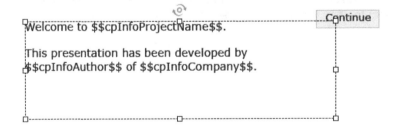

15. Preview the project. If the text does not appear in the text caption, you will most likely need to close the preview and resize the text caption. (If you are sure that the text caption is large enough, you may need to replace the variable text that is not appearing with a variable with a larger Maximum length.)

16. Close the preview and then save your work.

User Variables

As you've seen, variables serves two main roles: store data and, if you'd like, display the stored data within text captions.

You're going to leverage a variable's ability to store and display data to give learners the illusion that your eLearning course was customized just for them. If your learners type their name into a Text Entry Box (TEB), they'll see their name on subsequent slides throughout the project.

In the activities that follow, you're going to create a User variable called **learner_name**. You'll attach the **learner_name** variable to a TEB. The name learners type into the TEB will be stored by the variable for as long as the lesson remains open. You'll also insert the **learner_name** variable within some text captions throughout the project. The stored variable data will appear in any text captions that include the **learner_name** variable. Cool stuff, right? Let's get it done.

Guided Activity 16: Create a User Variable

1. Ensure that the **VariableWidgetMe** project is still open.

2. Create a user variable.

   ☐ choose **Project > Variables**

   The Variables dialog box opens. You use this dialog box to create, edit, and update variables.

   ☐ from the **Type** drop-down menu, choose **User** (if necessary)

   ☐ click the **Add New** button at the right of the dialog box and, in the **Name** field, type **learner_name**

   When naming the new variable, you can use any of the following formats: LearnerName, learner_name, or learnerName. The format you choose is up to you, but you should be consistent, and you cannot use spaces.

   ☐ in the Value field, type **Learner**

   Although it is not a requirement to add a Value to every variable, it's a good idea to do so. By using a value of Learner for this variable, you are telling Captivate to display the name Learner if the learner does not type a name into the lesson as instructed.

   ☐ in the Description field type **This variable will gather the name of the learner so that it can be used throughout the lesson.**

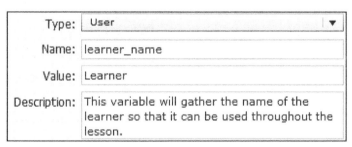

As with the Value field, a variable does not require a Description. However, including a Description saves you time and a headache down the road should you forget what the variable was supposed to do.

☐ click the **Save** button

The new variable appears at the bottom of the Variables dialog box.

☐ click the **Close** button

3. Save your work.

Guided Activity 17: Use a Variable to Gather Learner Data

1. Ensure that the **VariableWidgetMe** project is still open.

2. Add learner instructions on slide 2.

   ☐ go to slide **2**

   ☐ choose **Text > Text Caption**

   ☐ add the following text to the text caption: **Before we begin, let's learn a little more about you. Please type your first name into the space below. When you are done, press ENTER or click the Continue button.**

3. Resize and position the text caption until your slide looks similar to the picture below

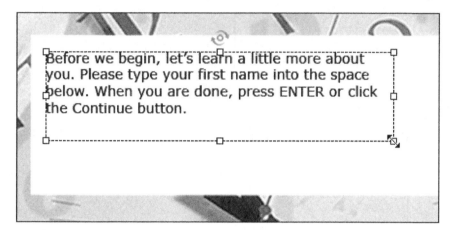

4. Save your work.

5. Insert a Text Entry Box.

   ☐ still working on slide 2, choose **Text > Text Entry Box**

   A small Text Entry Box has been added to the slide, along with a Submit button and a Hint caption. You will be editing the text on the button and removing the Hint caption soon.

6. Associate a user variable with the Text Entry Box.

   ☐ ensure that the **Text Entry Box** is selected

   ☐ on the **Properties Inspector**, **Style** tab, click the **Variable** drop-down menu and choose **learner_name**

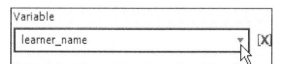

Now that the variable and the text entry box are associated, when a learner types anything into the text entry box, the information is stored by the learner_name variable until the lesson is closed. The stored data can be displayed within text captions throughout the lesson (provided the captions appear *after* the TEB slide, not before).

---

7. Set the Action for the Text Entry Box.

☐ on the **Properties Inspector**, select the **Actions** tab

☐ from the **On Success** drop-down menu, choose **Go to the next slide**

☐ ensure **Infinite Attempts** is selected

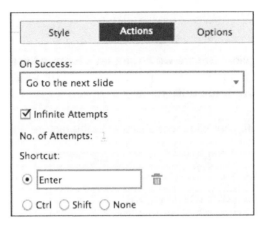

8. Remove the Hint caption.

☐ from the **Display** area, deselect **Hint**

User-Defined Variables Confidence Check

1. Resize and reposition the Text Entry Box and Submit button until your slide looks similar to the picture below.

2. Change the button's Caption to **Continue**.

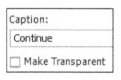

3. Go to slide **3** and insert the **learner_name** User variable into the text caption as shown in the picture below (when inserting the Variable, set the Maximum length to **100**).

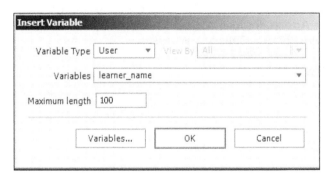

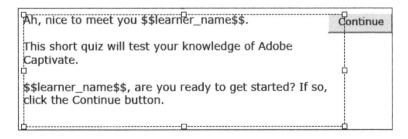

4. Preview the project. When you get to slide **2**, type your first name as instructed, and when you get to slide **3**... wait for it... MAGIC! The name you typed on slide **2** has been stored and now appears on slide **3**.

5. Close the preview and then save your work.

Widgets

Widgets are to Captivate what after-market accessories are to your car. For example, I purchased a car several years ago that included a standard AM/FM radio. I wanted satellite radio so I purchased an after-market device/widget that, when attached to my car radio, gives me access to satellite radio. Widgets add features to your project beyond those added by Adobe. To create a widget, you'll need to own a program like Adobe Animate (and know how to use the program far beyond the basic skill level). If you are not a widget developer (and I'm betting that you're not), you'll be happy to know that you can search the Internet for Captivate widgets (prices range from free to a few hundred dollars) and that several free widgets ship with Captivate.

There are three types of widgets: **Static** (not interactive and only display information), **Interactive** (change their appearance or function based on user input), and **Question** (allow you to add new question types to your project).

During the next few activities, you will be inserting a few free widgets, exploring which parts of the widget can be configured, and learning which properties are beyond your control (unless, of course, you are one of the aforementioned Animate developers).

Guided Activity 18: Insert and Format a Widget

1. Ensure that the **VariableWidgetMe** project is still open.

2. Insert the emailIcon widget.

   ☐ go to the last slide of the project (slide **10**)

   ☐ choose **Insert > Widget**

   The **Open** dialog box appears and you should be in the Captivate **Widgets** folder. (If not, navigate to the folder where Captivate is installed on your computer (for PC users, this is typically **C:\Program Files > Adobe**; for Mac users, this is typically in the **Applications** folder). Open **Adobe Captivate 2019 > Gallery > Widgets**.)

   ☐ open the **emailIcon.swf** widget

   The Widget Properties dialog box opens.

   ☐ in the **Label** field, change the **Label** to **Email**

   ☐ in the To field, type **biff.bifferson@supersimplisticsolutions.com**

   ☐ in the Subject line, type **I'd like more information about your products and services.**

   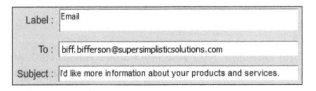

   ☐ change the Family to **Verdana**

❏ ensure that the Style is **Regular**

❏ change the Size to **13**

❏ click the **OK** button

Widget Confidence Check

1. Drag the widget until its slide position is similar to the image below

2. With the widget selected, use the Timing Inspector to change the widget's Display Timing to **Rest of Slide**.

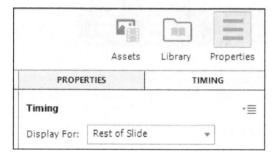

3. Preview the project. When you get to the last slide, click the Email icon.

   Your email program should start. Notice that the email is already addressed and that the subject line is filled in.

4. Close the email without sending or saving it.

5. Return to Captivate and close the preview.

6. Save and close the project.

7. Open **PerpetuateMe** from the **Captivate2019BeyondData** folder.

8. On slide **1**, insert the **PerpetualButton_AS3** widget. (Review the instruction that appears and then click the **OK** button.)

9. On the **Timing** Inspector, change the **Timing** for the widget to **Display For** time to **Rest of Project**.

NOTES

10. Still on slide **1**, move the **PerpetualButtons** widget to the lower right of the slide as shown in the picture below.

Now for the coolness of Perpetual buttons...

11. Preview the project.

    As the first slide fades in, notice that the button appears as a single, right-facing button.

12. Click the button on slide **1** to go to the next slide.

    Hopefully, you'll appreciate that Perpetual buttons include a Go to next slide action that automatically moves you through the presentation (but that's not the coolest part of Perpetual buttons).

13. Keep moving through the presentation. Once you get past the first slide (where the button was pointing right), notice that the button automatically gets forward and back arrows. When you reach the last slide, the button changes again and becomes a single, left-facing button. *Cool! Cool! Cool!*

    The trick to getting the Perpetual button to work? I'm not going to lie to you and say you could make your own button (widget) in a snap. In reality, you'd need experience with Adobe Animate. However, importing the widget and displaying it for the entire project (as you did during step 9 above) are what make the widget visible for the entire project.

14. Close the preview.

15. Save and close the project.

    Note: While cool, many widgets are Adobe Flash (SWF) objects and are **not HTML5-compliant** (meaning that they will not work for mobile learners or for learners where Flash is blocked by their corporate IT). You should not use SWFs in your project if you plan to support mobile learners and/or publish as HTML5. You can check a project for HTML5 compliance issues at any time by choosing **Project > HTML5 Tracker**. Anything flagged by the HTML5 Tracker should be removed from published projects intended to be used on mobile devices.

iCONLOGiC

"Skills and Drills" Learning

Module 4: Interactive Videos and Virtual Reality

In This Module You Will Learn About:

And You Will Learn To:

Interactive Videos

I'm a huge fan of incorporating videos into eLearning projects. In my experience, videos offer a higher level of learner interest and knowledge retention than text and/or images alone. However, as much as I love videos, I'm not happy with a major video limitation—a lack of learner interactivity. Sure, learners can stop, rewind, and fast-forward through most videos, but those abilities hardly equate to interactivity or engagement.

Captivate allows for videos (any videos) to include a high level of interactivity via knowledge checks, learner interactions, and more. You can insert bookmarks and jump learners to the marks from any point in the video or from other Captivate slides. You can also create overlay slides that will appear on the video. The overlay slides can be regular content slides or Knowledge Check slides.

Guided Activity 19: Insert an Interactive Video

1. Open **InteractiveVideoMe** from the Captivate2019BeyondData folder.

   The project contains two Knowledge Check questions. (Knowledge Check questions can be added to the project via the Quiz menu.)

2. Insert a blank slide for the video.

   ☐ choose **Insert > New Slide from > Blank**

   ☐ on the **Filmstrip**, drag the new slide above the first Knowledge Check slide

3. Add an interactive video.

   ☐ select the blank slide (slide **1**) and, on the toolbar, click **Interactive Video**

The Insert Video dialog box opens. You can either target an existing YouTube video or import a file from your computer. I have a video for you that will work perfectly.

☐ select **From your Computer**

☐ click the **Browse** button

☐ navigate to **Captivate2019BeyondData > images_videos**

☐ open **ScienceOfBoostering**

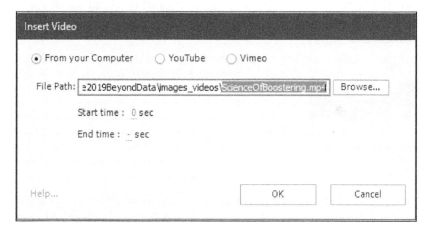

☐ click the **OK** button

The video is added to the slide.

Guided Activity 20: Add Bookmarks

1. Ensure that the **InteractiveVideoMe** project is still open (and that you've added the interactive video to the slide).

2. Add a Bookmark.

   ☐ on the **Filmstrip**, select slide **1**

   ☐ on the **Timeline**, position the Playhead at **35.5** seconds (you can check your exact timing via the information below the Timeline)

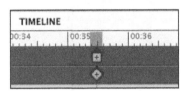

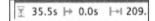

On the Timeline, notice that there are two icons underneath the Playhead: a square and a diamond. The square allows you to add bookmarks; the diamond allows you to add slide overlays. You'll add bookmarks first and then use the overlay feature to target the two Knowledge Check slides already in the project.

   ☐ click the square just below the Playhead

   ☐ name the Bookmark **Knowledge Check 1** and click the check mark

Note: You can delete a Bookmark at any time by clicking the **Trash** icon to the right of the Bookmark name.

A Bookmark can be used as a target for any jumps you'd like to make throughout the video or, as I like to use them, as breadcrumbs that keep me from getting lost in a large video.

Bookmarks Confidence Check

1. Add another bookmark at **2:58.5** on the Timeline (the area below the Timeline will display **178.5**) and name it **Knowledge Check 2**.

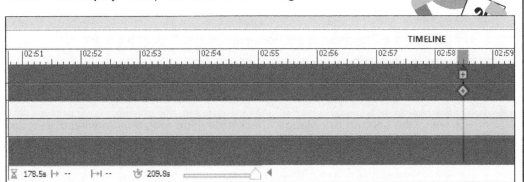

2. Save your work.

Guided Activity 21: Add Slide Overlays

1. Ensure that the **InteractiveVideoMe** project is still open.

2. Add a slide overlay.

   ☐ position the **Playhead** at the Bookmark you added to **35.5** mark

   ☐ click the **Insert Overlay** icon (the diamond beneath the Playhead)

   The **Overlay** dialog box opens.

   ☐ select the **second** Knowledge Check slide (How long after training does it take before most learning is forgotten?)

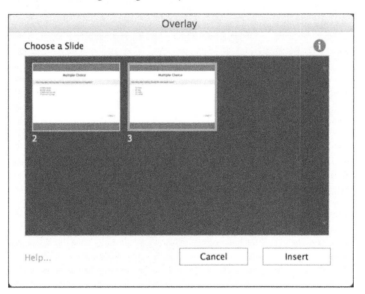

   ☐ click the **Insert** button

   On the **Filmstrip**, notice that the Knowledge Check slide thumbnail is a bit smaller, includes an **overlay icon,** and is slightly indented beneath the thumbnail for slide 1.

   Note: You can easily swap an overlay slide for another or remove the overlay effect by clicking the **Overlay** icon on the **Timeline** and either clicking **Choose Overlay Slide** or **Unlink Current Overlay Slide**.

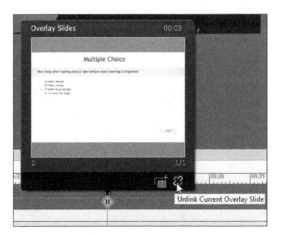

Overlays Confidence Check

1. Add the second Knowledge Check to the video on slide 1 as an overlay slide at the **2:58.5** bookmark.

2. Save your work.

3. Preview the project as **HTML5 in Browser**.

   As the video plays, you'll see (and be able to interact with) your two Knowledge Checks at the **35.5** and **2:58.5** mark respectively.

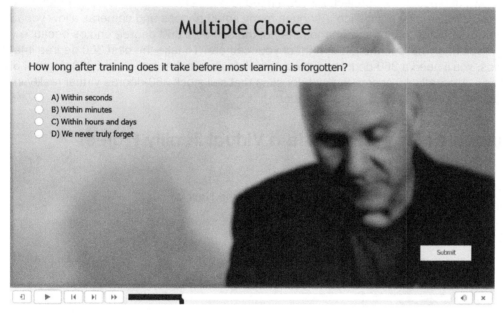

4. Close the browser and return to Captivate.

   You can control how see-through an overlay is on the Properties Inspector. And if you don't want an overlay, you can delete it by clicking its instance on the Timeline (you can also change an overlay to any other slide in the project so long as the slide isn't already being used as an overlay).

5. On the Timeline, select the Overlay icon at **35.5**.

6. On the Properties Inspector, change the **Background Opacity** to **30%.**

7. Preview the project as **HTML5 in Browser**.

   When the first overlay slide appears this time, notice that the background is lighter than before. If you wanted to remove the background completely and just show the overlay, you'd set the Opacity to 100%.

8. Close the browser and return to Captivate.

9. Change the background Opacity for the **35.5** second overlay back to **10%**.

10. Preview the project as **HTML5 in Browser** to see your changes.

11. **Save** your work and **close** the project.

NOTES

Virtual Reality

In my experience, students learn best when a course is relevant, engaging, and interactive. Virtual Reality (VR) is an interactive three-dimensional environment/simulation that can be controlled by the learner's body or a computer mouse.

With Captivate, you can easily, and I mean easily, create VR projects using 360-degree photos or videos. During the next few activities, you'll import a few 360 images into a new VR project.The images, which are free to use, are a gift from Adobe (via Assets).

I would expect that once you've played around with the Captivate's VR features, you'll want to add your own 360 assets to a project. All you'll need to get started is a camera. Unfortunately, your phone's camera may not suffice. Although many smart phones and cameras allow you take panoramic photos, panoramic images are not the same as 360-degree photos because you're only capturing what's to the left or right of your camera. To take the best 360 degree images or videos, you'll need a 360-degree camera or tools/software that can output 360-degree, 3D images. Alternatively, search the web for sites that sell stock 360-degree virtual reality images (there are several vendors, including Adobe).

Guided Activity 22: Create a Virtual Reality Project

1. Create a new Virtual Reality project.

   ❑ on Captivate's Welcome screen, click the **New** tab

   ❑ double-click **Virtual Reality Project**

   If this is your first time creating a Virtual Reality Project, Adobe creates a new sample project for you (instead of a typical blank project). If the sample VR project was created for you, close it (there is no need to save if prompted) and then double-click Virtual Reality Project on the Welcome screen again.

2. Add a 360 image to the project.

   ❑ from the middle of the new project's lone slide, click **Add 360 Image/Video**

   ❑ if necessary, navigate to the **Adobe Captivate 2019** application folder

   ❑ open the **Gallery** folder

   ❑ from the **360BGAssets** folder, open **Kidslab.jpg**

Although the image onscreen appears to be just another image, it's actually a 360-degree image. There aren't yet any interactive areas, but you can move around the virtual room by dragging your mouse (there's no need to preview the project). Go ahead and give it a try.

3. Save the project to the Captivate2019BeyondData folder as **MyVirtualReality**.

Guided Activity 23: Add a Text Hotspot

1. Ensure that the **MyVirtualReality** project is open.

2. Add a text hotspot.

   ☐ drag around the virtual room until your orientation is similar to the image below (you're going to add a target hotspot to the monitor in front of the two green chairs)

   ☐ on the toolbar, click **Hotspots** and choose **Target**

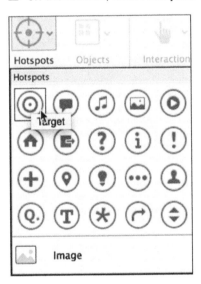

   ☐ drag the Target icon just to the right of the monitor

3. Set the Action for the Hotspot to display text.

   ☐ double-click the Target hotspot to open the **Properties** inspector

   ☐ on the **Actions** > **On Click** drop-down menu, choose **Display Text**

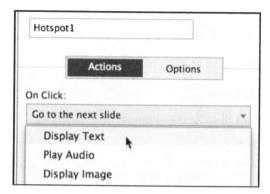

   ☐ type **20 new computers were purchased for the lab in August. Each system has 64GB of RAM and a 2TB solid state drive.**

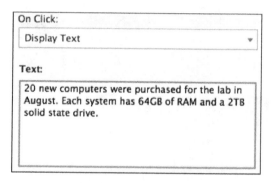

4. Preview the project.

5. Click the **Target** hotspot so see the text appear in its own window.

6. Click away from the Target hotspot.

   A green check mark appears which indicates that the interactive area has been viewed.

7. Close the Preview.

8. Save your work.

NOTES

Guided Activity 24: Recolor a Hotspot

1. Ensure that the **MyVirtualReality** project is open.

2. Recolor a hotspot.

   ☐ double-click the Target hotspot that you previously added to the slide

   Double-clicking the hotspot makes it possible to change its colors.

   ☐ click once on any **black area** of the hotspot

   ☐ on the **Properties** Inspector, click the **Fill** drop-down menu

   ☐ select **any Fill color** you like

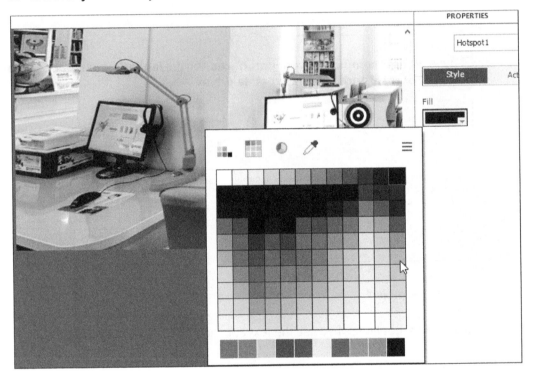

Guided Activity 25: Add an Audio Hotspot

1. Ensure that the **MyVirtualReality** project is open.

2. Add an Audio hotspot.

   ☐ on the slide, drag the virtual room until you're in a position similar to what is shown below.

   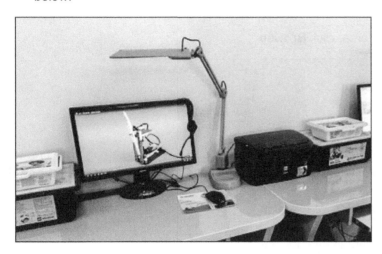

   ☐ on the toolbar, click **Hotspots** and choose **Audio**

   ☐ drag the Audio icon just below the lamp as shown below

   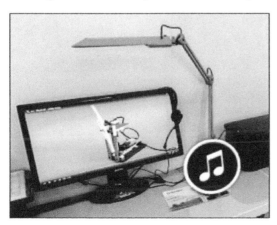

3. Select music to play if the hotspot is selected.

   ❑ double-click the **Audio** hotspot to open the **Properties** inspector

   ❑ on the **Actions** tab, **On Click** drop-down menu, choose **Play Audio**

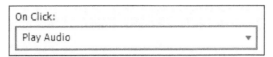

   ❑ from the **Audio** area, click **Browse**

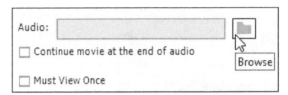

   ❑ from **Captivate2019BeyondData > audio** folder open **BeethovenSymphony9**

4. Preview the project.

5. Click the Audio hotspot to hear the music.

   Note: If you wanted to allow the learner to stop audio files from playing, add another hotspot and set its Action to **Stop Triggered Audio**.

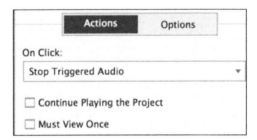

6. Close the Preview.

Hotspots Confidence Check

1. Pan up so you can see the ceiling.

2. Insert a **Text Label** on the ceiling with the following Label text: **Why are you looking up here?**

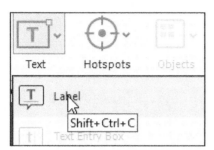

3. You have limited font formatting controls for Text Labels. Select any font formats and colors that you like.

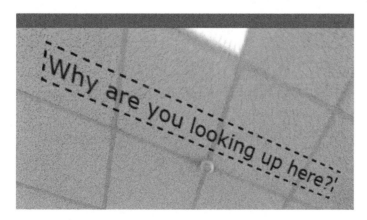

Guided Activity 26: Add a Quiz to a Virtual Reality Project

1. Ensure that the **MyVirtualReality** project is open.

2. Add Question Slides.

   ☐ orient yourself in the room similar to what is shown in the image below

   ☐ on the toolbar, click **Hotspots** and choose **Help**

   ☐ position the Help icon similar to what is shown below

   ☐ double-click the **Help** hotspot to open the **Properties** inspector

   ☐ click **Add Questions**

   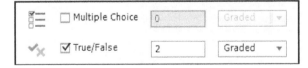

   The Insert Questions dialog box opens.

   ☐ select **True/False**

   ☐ change the number of questions to **2**

   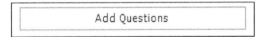

   ☐ click the **OK** button

3. Edit the first Question Slide.

   ☐ on the **Filmstrip**, select slide **2**

   ☐ change the question to **300 new laptops were added in August.**

   ☐ select False as the correct answer

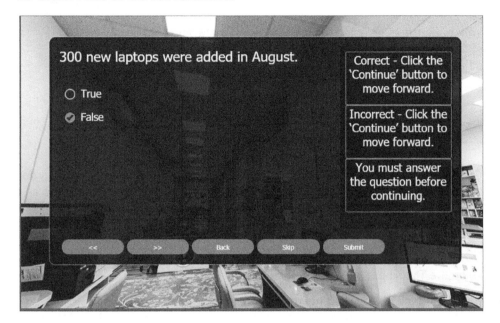

4. Edit the second Question Slide.

   ☐ on the **Filmstrip**, select slide **3**

   ☐ change the question to **All new computers have solid state drives.**

   ☐ select True as the correct answer

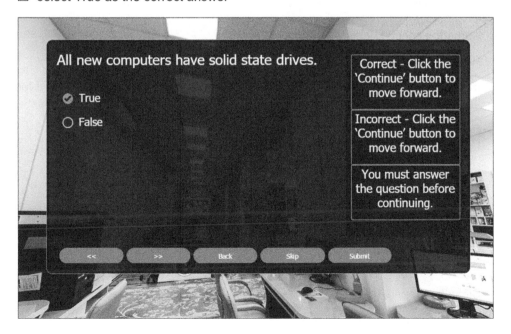

NOTES

Virtual Reality Confidence Check

1. Preview the project and take the quiz.

2. When finished, close the preview and return to the Captivate project.

3. On the Filmstrip, select slide 1.

4. With no hotspots selected, notice that there are two navigation options on the Properties Inspector: Guided and Exploratory. By default, Exploratory is selected.

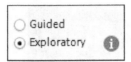

Guided: the learner is taken from one hotspot to another automatically. The order of the hotspots is based on their order on the Timeline (the lower down the Timeline an object appears, the sooner it appears onscreen). **Exploratory**: The learner manually moves around the room and interacts with hotspots.

5. On the Properties Inspector, select **Guided**.

6. Open the Timeline.

7. Select the bottom (last) hotspot on the Timeline.

8. On the Properties Inspector, name the hotspot **Computers**.

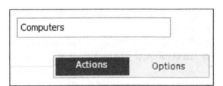

9. Name the second hotspot **Music**.

10. Name the third hotspot **Quiz**.

Based on the current Timeline order, the first thing you should see in a Guided lesson is the Computer hotspot, then the Music hotspot, and then the Quiz.

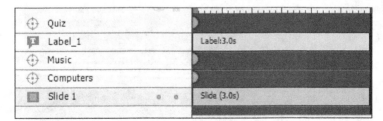

11. Preview the project and notice how you are guided through the lesson.

12. Close the Preview.

13. On the Timeline, drag the Computers hotspot above the Music hotspot.

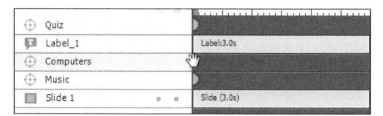

14. Preview the project again and this time you should be taken to the music hotspot first.

15. Close the preview (you do not have to wait for the music to stop playing).

16. On the **Timeline**, drag the **Music** hotspot above the **Computer** hotspot.

17. Preview the project to see the changed navigation.

18. Close the preview.

19. On the Properties Inspector, select **Exploratory**.

20. Select slide 1, click the **Slides** tool and choose **360 Slide**.

21. On slide **4**, import the **Cafe** 360 image from Captivate's **360BGAssets** folder.

22. Back on slide **1**, add a **Navigation Hotspot** and position over the first door.

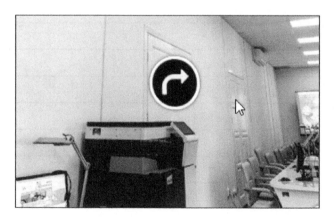

23. Ensure that the On Click Action for the Navigation Hotspot is **Go to the next slide**.

24. Preview the project and click the Navigation Hotspot.

    The two question slides on the Filmstrip are overlay slides, not standard slides. Normally, **Go to the next slide** would go to the question slides. Because overlay slides are ignored when it comes to slide navigation, you go directly to slide 4.

25. Close the preview.

26. Spend a few moments adding random hotspots and text to the cafe slide.

27. Preview your changes.

28. When finished, close the preview, save your work, and close the project.

Notes

iCONLOGiC

"Skills and Drills" Learning

Module 5: Interactions

In This Module You Will Learn About:

- Learning Interactions, page 72

- Drag and Drop, page 76

- Change State Actions, page 96

- Drag and Drop Assets, page 104

And You Will Learn To:

Learning Interactions

Interactions, also referred to as Smart Learning Interactions, are powerful widgets that allow you to quickly insert interactive objects onto a slide. Captivate ships with a wide range of Interactions, such as Process Cycles and Pyramids, and you can download others. As you work with Interactions, you'll find that you can customize not only the content but also the look and feel of the Interaction.

Guided Activity 27: Insert a Process Circle

1. Open **InteractMe** from the Captivate2019BeyondData folder.

2. Insert an Interaction on slide 2.

    ☐ on the Filmstrip, select slide **2**

    ☐ on the toolbar, click **Interactions** and choose **Learning Interactions**

The **Select Interaction** dialog box opens.

    ☐ select **Process Circle**

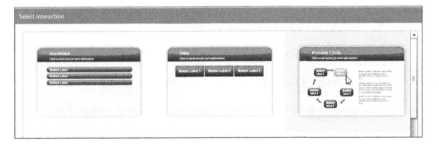

    ☐ click the **Insert** button

The **Configure interaction** dialog box opens.

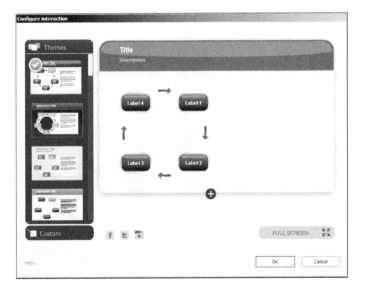

3. Select a Theme.

   ❑ with the Configure Interactions dialog box still open, scroll down the list of **Themes** and select **Theme 15 Green**

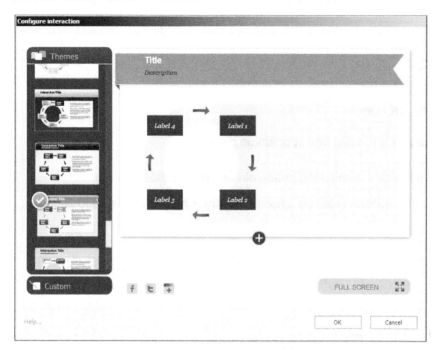

4. Add a Title and Description.

   ❑ double-click the word **Title** to select it and then replace it with: **Top Chocolate Bars**

   Note: When attempting to select Learning Interactions text, you might find that it takes more than a few clicks to select text. I've seen it take six, seven, even eight clicks to highlight text (sometimes just two). I don't know why there is such "click inconsistency" in this area of Captivate, but know that it's not you... and keep on clicking.

   ❑ select the word **Description** and replace it with: **Based on international sales.**

5. Add Label text.

   ❑ select **Label 1** to make it the active label

   ❑ select the phrase **Label 1** and replace it with your favorite chocolate bar

6. Add Button Content.

❑ just to the right of the label you just edited, select the **Button Content 1**

❑ replace the text with a description of the chocolate bar you typed into the label field

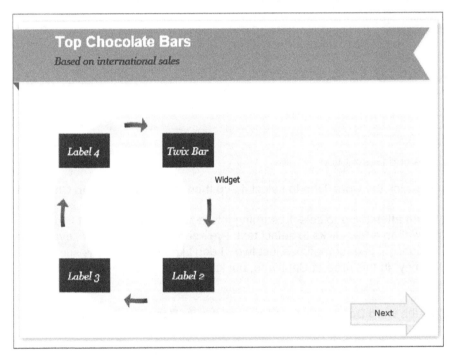

❑ click the **OK** button

The Interaction is created and appears on slide **2**.

7. Send the Interaction behind the button already on the slide.

❑ with the Interaction selected, choose **Modify > Arrange > Send to Back**

8. If you'd like, resize the interaction a bit so there's a bit more white space around the interaction (if you resize the interaction while pressing [**shift**] on your keyboard, you'll be able to resize proportionally).

9. Test the Interaction.

❑ choose **Preview > Project**

When you get to slide 2, click the candy bar label you added, and its description appears. When you click the other labels, they spin into view. How awesome is that?

10. Close the Preview.

Interactions Confidence Check

1. Double-click the Interaction to reopen the Widget Properties dialog box.

2. Replace the remaining labels with your favorite candy bars and descriptions.

3. Preview the Project and test the Interaction.

4. Close the preview.

5. Reopen the Widget Properties dialog box.

6. At the left of the dialog box, click Custom.

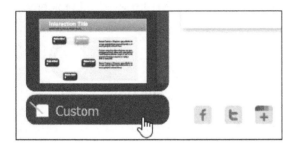

7. From the Themes area, click Customize.

8. Spend a few moments changing the attributes of the Buttons, Content, and Header.

   Note: Unlike the SWF widgets you inserted during the last module, Learning Interactions won't be flagged by the HTML5 Tracker as being on-HTML5 compliant. Learners should have no problem using the Interactions on mobile devices.

9. When finished, save and close the project.

Drag and Drop

Few things fully engage the learner more than interactivity. And allowing learners to move things around the screen—dragging and dropping—is at, or near, the top of the hill when it comes to creating meaningful interactivity.

During activities in this section, you will learn how to create a drag and drop interaction and how to fully customize the drag and drop experience with unique sources, targets, and clever naming and formatting of buttons and feedback messages as you complete a soft-skills lesson on appropriate work attire.

Guided Activity 28: Create a Sorting Drag and Drop Interaction

1. Open **DragAndDropBasicsBegin** from the Captivate2019BeyondData folder.

2. Start the Drag and Drop Wizard.

   ☐ go to slide **2**

   ☐ on the toolbar, click **Interactions** and choose **Drag and Drop**

   The Drag and Drop Interaction Wizard opens.

3. Specify drag sources.

   ☐ at the **right** of the slide, click once on each colorful rectangle and the colorful square

   ☐ click on a white area of the slide background to deselect any selected slide objects

   Notice that both rectangles and the square shapes have a green border, indicating that each is now a **drag source**. A drag source is an object that can be dragged by the learner. Next to each drag source is a red **minus sign** that can be used to remove an object as a drag source.

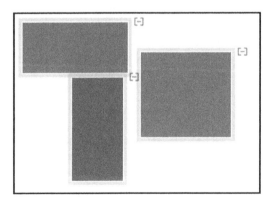

4. Create a drag source "type," or category.

❐ press [**shift**] on your keyboard and then select each colored rectangle to reselect them

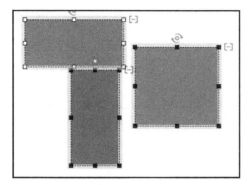

❐ release the [**shift**] key

❐ at the top of the **Drag and Drop Interaction Wizard**, click the **plus sign**

The **Add new type** dialog box opens.

❐ replace the existing text with the word **Rectangles**

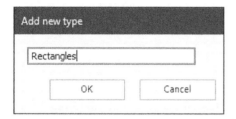

❐ click the **OK** button

The selected shapes have been assigned to a group called **Rectangles**. In a moment you'll assign the three rectangles on the slide to a **Drop Area**. Grouping the drag objects together as you've just done will make this potential chore go faster (when you assign a drag group to a Drop Area, all group items get assigned to the Drop Area at one time).

5. Create a second drag source type.

❐ still working on step 1 of the Wizard, click once on each of the colorful ovals to specify them as drag sources

❐ ensure all three ovals are selected and then click the **Add to type plus sign** to add a new type

❐ name the new group **Ovals**

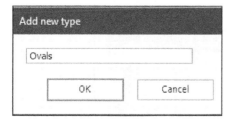

❐ click the **OK** button

NOTES

6. Specify Drop Targets.

❑ at the upper right of the **Drag and Drop Interaction Wizard**, click the **Next** button

You are now on step 2 of 3 of the Drag and Drop Wizard.

❑ click once on the large, black **square**

❑ click once on the large, black **circle**

Both objects now have blue borders indicating that they are now **Drop Targets**. As with Drag Sources, you can remove an object as a Drop Target by clicking the **red minus sign**.

7. Map drag sources to correct drag targets.

❑ at the upper right of the **Drag and Drop Interaction Wizard**, click the **Next** button

You are now on step 3 of 3.

❑ from the middle of any one of the colorful **rectangles**, drag the **correct solution** icon (the icon in the middle of each drag source, shown in the image below) to the square target

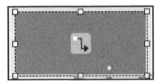

Blue arrows connect all of the objects in the Rectangles group to the target. The black square has now been identified as the correct answer for the rectangles.

❑ from the middle of any one of the colorful **ovals**, drag the **correct solution** icon to the black circle

The circle has been specified as the correct answer for all of the ovals. Your slide should look like this:

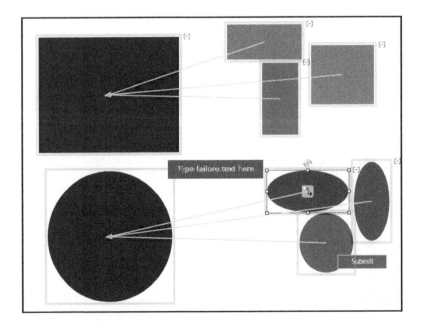

8. Finish the Drag and Drop Interaction Wizard.

    ☐ on the **Drag and Drop Interaction Wizard**, click the **Finish** button

9. Preview the Project

10. Drag each of the rectangles to the square target, and each of the circles to the oval target.

11. Click the **Submit** button.

    The Success caption appears in the center of the screen.

12. On the playbar at the bottom of the Preview window, click the **Rewind** button.

    You are returned to the title slide, then when you re-enter your drag and drop slide, the drag and drop has been reset.

13. Drag the source objects again, but this time drag the ovals and rectangle shapes to the wrong drop areas.

14. Click the **Submit** button so see a Failure caption.

    Although the drag and drop interaction is working, there are a few problems. First, the position of the Submit button needs to be moved so it isn't covering any of the ovals.

    Second, the Failure and Success captions contain placeholder text that you'll need to replace with "real" text.

    Third, if the learner changes his or her mind after dragging an object onto a target, an Undo button would be nice.

    You'll fix these three pesky issues next.

15. Close the Preview.

Guided Activity 29: Manage Drag and Drop Buttons

1. Ensure that the **DragAndDropBasicsBegin** project is still open.

   Notice that there is a new inspector at the right of the window: Drag and Drop. (If the Drag and Drop inspector isn't on your screen—it usually appears automatically—choose **Window > Drag and Drop**.)

2. Add and organize drag and drop buttons.

   ☐ on the **Drag and Drop inspector**, **Actions**, **Buttons** area (at the bottom of the Inspector), select **Undo** and **Reset**

   Undo and Reset buttons appear on your slide.

   ☐ select all three buttons (you can use [**shift**]-click to select all three)

   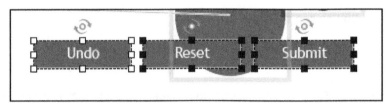

   ☐ using the **down arrow key** on your keyboard, "nudge" the buttons straight down until they are clear of the source objects

   Note: Press and hold any one of the arrow keys on your keyboard to move the buttons continuously; press [**shift**] on your keyboard and any one of the arrow keys together to move the buttons **twice as fast**.

   ☐ with the buttons still selected, nudge them to the right (right arrow key) until they align with the farthest right drag source

   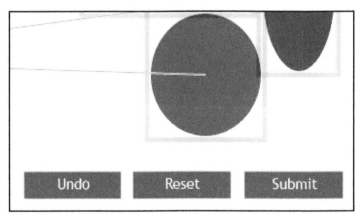

3. Write success and failure caption text and re-position captions.

   ❏ in the center of the slide, drag the success caption away from the failure caption

   ❏ change the text in the success caption to **Good job! That is correct!**

   ❏ change the text in the failure caption to **Oops! Not quite right!**

   ❏ move **both captions** to a location on your slide that looks good to you

   Note: Because the Success and Failure captions will never be displayed to the learner at the same time, they can be positioned on top of each other if you'd like.

4. Test the Undo, Reset, and Submit buttons and view the new caption text.

   ❏ Preview the Project

   ❏ drag one source object onto a target

   ❏ click the **Undo** button

   The drag source object is returned to its original position.

   ❏ drag several sources onto targets

   ❏ click the **Undo** button

   Notice that only the most recent drag action is undone.

   ❏ drag several source objects to targets

   ❏ click the **Reset** button

   The Reset button moves all source objects to their original positions. But check out what happens if the learner clicks the Submit button.

   ❏ drag several, or all, of the source objects to targets (wrong or right, it doesn't matter at this point)

   ❏ click the **Submit** button

   Because the interaction is basically a quiz question, your drag and drop answer is "graded," judged right or wrong, and you see either the Success caption or the Failure caption. However, notice that the Undo or Reset buttons disappear after you submit an answer. What if you want to allow your learners to try the interaction again?

   ❏ on the Playbar, click the **Rewind** button

   You return to slide 1 and then, when you re-enter slide 2, the drag and drop interaction is reset. To ensure that your learners know how to try the interaction again, you could tell them to click the Rewind button to get another chance. A better option is to add a Retry button directly to the slide.

5. Close the Preview window.

6. Create a retry button.

   ❏ from the toolbar, click **Interactions** and choose **Button**

   A new button appears in the center of the slide.

☐ drag the new button to align to the left of your **Undo** button

☐ if necessary, open the **Properties** inspector

☐ on the **Properties** inspector, **Style** tab, change the **Caption** to **Retry**

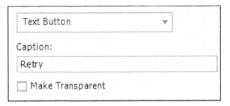

☐ on the **Properties** inspector, **Actions** tab, **On Success** drop-down menu, choose **Go to the previous slide**

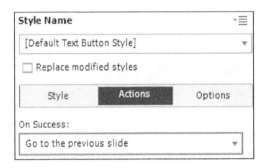

7. Apply a matching style to a button.

☐ with the **Retry** button still selected, from the **Properties** inspector, **Style Name** drop-down menu, choose **Default Quiz Button Style**

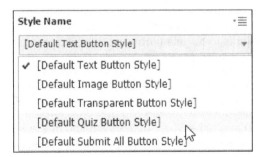

8. Align and resize the Retry button as necessary to align it with the existing buttons.

Basic Drag and Drop Confidence Check

1. Preview the Project, play with the interaction, and then and try the **Retry** button. (Clicking Retry takes you to the first slide, which resets the interaction.)

2. Close the Preview window and, on the **Drag and Drop** inspector, **Actions** tab, select **Infinite Attempts**.

3. Preview the project, do the interaction **incorrectly**, then click **Submit**.

   After clicking **Submit**, you still have access to every button, *and* you can keep trying the interaction until you position everything correctly. However, once you drag everything to the correct areas and click **Submit**, the **Undo** and **Reset** buttons disappear.

   As you've seen, clicking the **Retry** button takes the learner back to slide 1 *and* resets the interaction (this navigation is necessary because an interaction cannot reset without first leaving the current slide and then returning). It would be more elegant if it felt like clicking the **Retry** button simply reset the current slide instead of leaving the current slide, displaying slide 1, and then returning. You'll learn a bit of trickery in the next activity that gives the illusion of staying on the same slide, all while the learner leaves and returns.

4. Close the Preview.

5. Select the **Retry** button and, on the **Properties** inspector, deselect **Infinite Attempts** and ensure that the No. of Attempts is **1**.

6. Save your work.

NOTES

Guided Activity 30: Create a "Trick" Reset Interaction Slide

1. Ensure that the **DragAndDropBasicsBegin** project is still open.

2. Duplicate a drag and drop slide.

   ☐ on the **Filmstrip**, right-click the drag and drop slide (slide **2**) and choose **Duplicate**

3. Remove the drag and drop interaction from slide 3.

   ☐ ensure you're working on the duplicate slide (slide **3**)

   ☐ on the **Drag and Drop** inspector, to the right of the **Interaction_2** title area, click the **Delete Interaction** icon (the trash can)

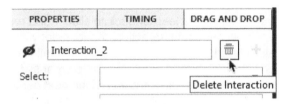

4. Remove the remaining button.

   ☐ ensure you're working on the duplicate slide (slide **3**)

   ☐ select and delete the **Retry** button

5. Adjust Object timing.

   ☐ ensure you're working on the duplicate slide (slide **3**)

   ☐ on the **Timeline**, select all of the object bars

   ☐ on the **Timeline**, right-click the selected objects and choose **Show for the rest of the slide**

   ☐ on the **Timeline**, shorten the slide's duration to approximately **0.2** seconds

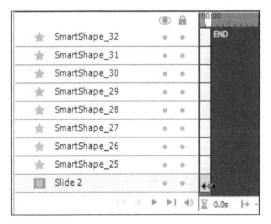

6. Reorder slides.

   ☐ on the **Filmstrip**, drag slide **3** above slide 2

7. Preview the project.

8. Try the drag and drop interaction and Submit your answer.

9. Click the **Retry** button.

   After clicking the **Retry** button, instead of seeing the title slide, you stayed on slide 3, *and* the interaction was reset. However, staying on the slide 3 was an illusion. In reality, clicking the **Retry** button took you to the previous slide in the project (slide 2, which looks identical to slide 3). After a few tenths of a second on slide 2, you ended up back on slide 3 and the interaction was reset.

10. Save and close the project.

NOTES

Guided Activity 31: Explore an Advanced Drag and Drop Interaction

1. Open **DragDropMeDone** from the Captivate2019BeyondData folder.

2. Preview the project.

   At the left, say hello to James. At the right, notice some clothes. Your mission, should you choose to accept it, is to ensure that James is dressed appropriately for work.

3. Test the interaction.

   ☐ drag the **beer tee** to James' shirt area

   ☐ drag the **cut-off shorts** to the appropriate area on James

   ☐ drag either the **oxfords** or the **sandals** to the appropriate area on James

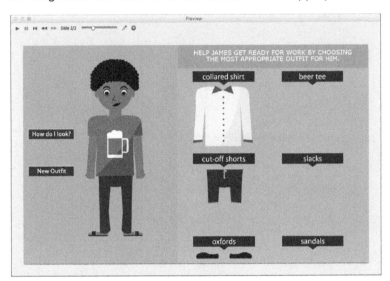

   ☐ at the left, click the **How do I look** button

   Because this particular ensemble isn't *quite* appropriate for work, you're prompted to try again. Not only that, but did you notice that the expression on James' face changed? That's a "state" in action; something you'll cover after tackling Drag and Drop.

   ☐ at the left, click the **New Outfit** button

   The slide is reset.

☐ drag the **collared shirt**, **slacks**, and **oxfords** to the appropriate area on James

☐ click the **How do I look** button

Because you have positioned the clothes correctly, the "I look sharp" caption appears. In addition, the expression on James' face reflects just how ready for work he is!

4. Close the preview.

5. Explore the drop zones.

☐ on the Filmstrip, select slide **2**

On James, notice that there are three smart shapes positioned strategically on his body. These shapes serve as drop zones for the clothing. Each of the shapes has been formatted with 0% opacity so they are see-through.

In the activities that follow, you'll build the interaction by targeting the three drop zones with specific items of clothing.

6. Explore the Drag and Drop Inspector.

☐ on the slide, select the **top drop zone** by clicking on James' chest

☐ at the right of the Captivate window, observe the **Drag and Drop** inspector, **Format** tab

There are several options on the **Format** tab that allow you to precisely control the drag and drop functionality. You'll be playing with some of these options soon.

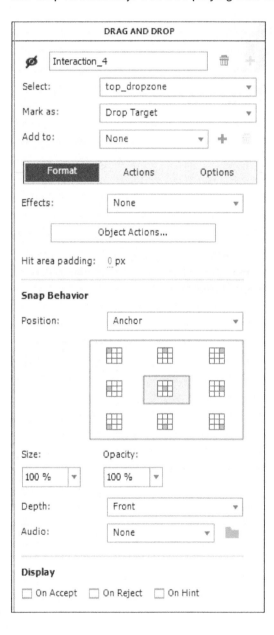

7. Close the project (there is no need to save it).

Guided Activity 32: Create an Advanced Drag and Drop Interaction

1. Open **DragDropMeStart** from the Captivate2019BeyondData folder.

2. Insert a Drag and Drop Interaction.

    ☐ select slide **2**

    ☐ change the **View Magnification** enough that you can see the entire slide (including all of the clothes at the right)

    ☐ on the toolbar, click **Interactions** and choose **Drag and Drop**

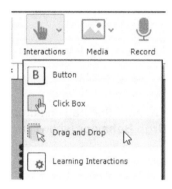

As you experienced earlier in this module, the **Drag and Drop Interaction Wizard** opens; you are on step 1 of 3.

☐ on the slide, click once on each of the six clothing items to specify them as **drag sources**

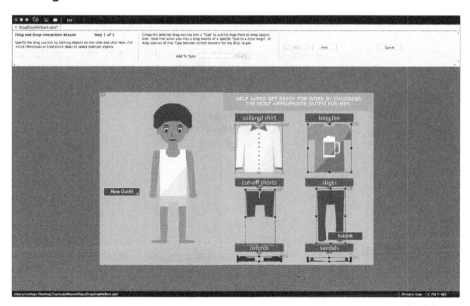

☐ at the upper right of the **Drag and Drop Interaction Wizard**, click the **Next** button

You are now on step 2 of 3. This screen allows you to specify the **Drop Targets**. For this lesson, the targets are the three smart shapes covering James.

NOTES

❏ on the slide, click each of the **three smart shapes** covering James' body

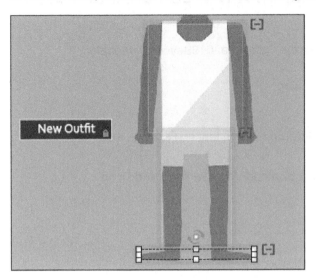

Note: Should you select an object accidentally, you can remove the drag and drop functionality from an object by clicking **Remove Drag-Drop Behavior** (shown in the image below).

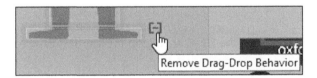

❏ at the upper right of the **Drag and Drop Interaction Wizard**, click the **Next** button

The third and final step allows you to associate **Drag Sources** with **Drop Targets**.

❏ on the slide, drag the **correct solution** icon in the middle of the **collared shirt** to the **top Drop Target**

❏ on the slide, drag the **correct solution** icon in the middle of the **slacks** to the **middle Drop Target**

❏ on the slide, drag the **correct solution** icon in the middle of the **oxfords** to the **bottom Drop Target**

3. Finish the Drag and Drop Interaction.

❏ at the upper right of the **Drag and Drop Interaction Wizard**, click the **Finish** button

Advanced Drag and Drop Confidence Check

1. Move the Submit button to the left of James and change the button caption to **How do I look?**

On the slide, there are two feedback captions (a green Success Smart Shape and, behind that, a Failure Smart Shape).

2. Drag the Success Caption out of the way.

3. Move the Failure Caption (the purple one) to the left of James' head.

4. Change its text to **That's not it. Click New Outfit to try again**.

5. Drag the **Success Caption** to the left of James' head.

6. Replace the Smart Shape with a **Cloud Callout Smart Shape** (right-click the caption, choose **Replace Smart Shape**, and then choose **Cloud Callout**).

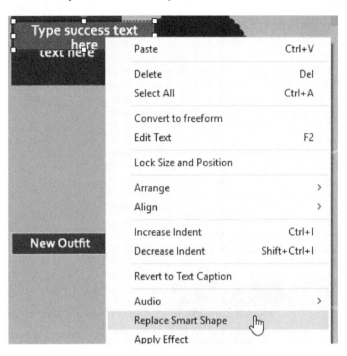

7. Change the text in the Smart Shape to **I look sharp!**

8. Drag the tail of the smart shape so it points to James' head.

9. Insert a **Reset** button by selecting **Reset** on the Drag and Drop Inspector, **Actions** tab.

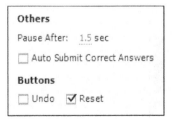

10. Change the caption on the Reset button to **New Outfit**.

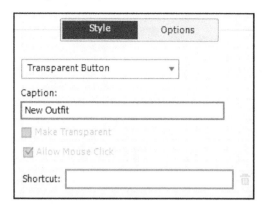

11. On the slide, position and resize the **New Outfit** button over the original **New Outfit** button.

    In the Drag and Drops Basics lesson, you learned that the Reset button resets the interaction at any point before you click the Submit button. You also learned that once you click the Submit button, the Reset button vanishes, and the only way to try again is to rewind to the previous slide and re-enter the Drag and Drop slide.

    To make it easier for your learners to "rewind" and try again, you created a Retry button and a "trick" retry slide to create the illusion that the Retry button didn't take the learner away from the slide.

    For this project, by naming the Reset button and the "trick" Retry button the same and placing them one over the other, you simplified the button for your learners. Learners will get the impression that they could simply try a new outfit at any time, whether they have already submitted an answer or not.

    You next need to ensure that clothing items do not end up on the wrong part of James' body. You'll accomplish the task via the Object Actions button on the Drag and Drop Inspector.

    Note: You might be wondering why I didn't just use the **Infinite Attempts** setting to allow repeated attempts to solve the interaction. The Infinite Attempts option eliminates the possibility of an On Failure action, which will be needed later to change the state of James' facial expression (as you saw in the finished sample).

12. Select the **top_dropzone** smart shape (the area where the collared shirt will go).

13. On the **Drag and Drop** inspector, select the **Format** tab.

14. Click **Object Actions**.

NOTES

15. On the **Accepted Drag Sources** dialog box, deselect everything except **Beer_Tee** and **Collared_Shirt**.

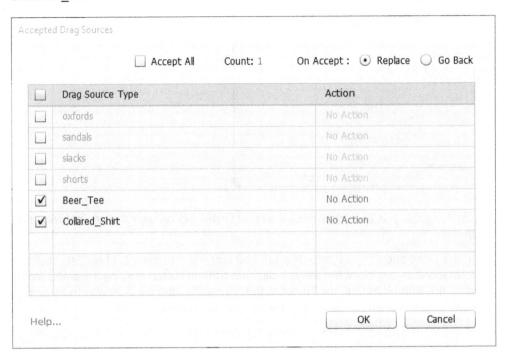

16. From the top of the dialog box, deselect **Accept All**.

17. Click the **Replace** button.

Notice how the **Count** at the top of the dialog box defaults to **1**. This is the number of items that will be accepted into a drop zone at one time and ensures that James can only wear one of the shirts at a time.

18. Click the **OK** button.

19. Modify the Object Actions for the middle Drop Zone (as shown below).

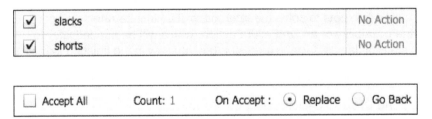

20. Modify the Object Actions for the third Drop Zone (as shown below).

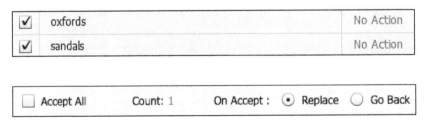

21. You're just about ready to test the interaction. Just before you do, select the **middle** Drop Zone (where the slacks will go).

    Because this drop zone is a bit narrow, you can add a bit of a grace area around any zone for those learners who might not be as precise with the mouse as others.

22. On the **Drag and Drop** Inspector, **Format** tab, change the **Hit area padding** to **100**.

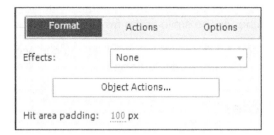

23. Preview the project.

24. Test the interaction.

    You should only be able to put specific items of clothing in each drop area. In addition, if you get within 100 pixels of the area where the slacks belong, the area will grab the item (you don't have to be perfect with your mouse... close enough is good enough).

25. Close the preview.

26. Save and close project.

Change State Actions

Here's one scenario: You've drawn a star shape on a slide and given it a Fill color of black. You'd like an interactive slide that lets the learner change the color of the star from black to blue when a corresponding button is clicked.

Here's another scenario: You've got two nearly identical characters on a slide. One character is smiling; the other character is frowning. Depending on how the learner interacts with your slide, you'd like the expression the learner sees to either be the smile or the frown.

Although both scenarios above seem complicated, you're about to learn that you can accomplish both tasks by using Captivate's **State View** and **Change State Actions**.

Guided Activity 33: Change States

1. Open **StateBasicsBegin** from the Captivate2019BeyondData folder.

2. Add States to a shape.

   ☐ go to slide **2** and select the **star** shape

   ☐ on the **Properties** inspector, click the **State View** button (shown highlighted in the image below)

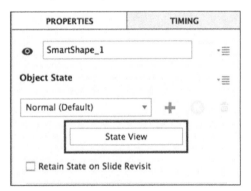

The Filmstrip is replaced with the **Object State** pane. There is currently one State in the view: Normal.

   ☐ on the Object State View, click the **New State** button

---

A dialog box opens.

❑ replace the placeholder text with the word **Blue**

❑ click the **OK** button

A new state named Blue appears on the Object State view below Normal.

❑ on the slide, the star should still be selected

❑ on the **Properties** inspector, **Style** tab, click the **Fill** drop-down menu and choose any blue Fill that you like

3. Close State View.

❑ on the toolbar, click the **Exit State** icon

Your screen returns to Filmstrip view.

4. Use an Action to change the State of an object.

❑ on the slide, select the button with the word **Blue**

❑ in the **Properties** inspector, **Actions** tab, **On Success** drop-down menu, choose **Change State of**

Note: The list of Actions is not alphabetical. You'll likely need to scroll down the Actions list to find **Change State of**.

❑ in the next drop-down menu, ensure that **Smartshape_1** is selected

❑ in the State drop-down menu, ensure that **Blue** is selected (this is the State you just created)

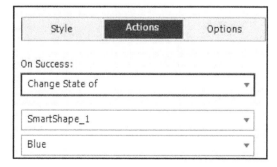

Change States Confidence Check

1. Preview the project.

2. Click the button with the word **Blue**.

   The appearance of the button changes from its Normal State (Black) to the Blue State.

3. Close the Preview window.

4. Add a New State to your star smart shape named **Red.**

5. The the Fill color for the **Red** State's star to **red**.

6. Exit State View.

7. Assign an Action to the Red button to change the State of the star shape to the Red State.

8. Assign an Action to the Normal button to change the state of the star shape back to the Normal State.

9. Preview the project and test the States by clicking each of the buttons.

10. Save and close the project.

Guided Activity 34: Use States to Swap Images

1. Open **StateMe** from the Captivate2019BeyondData folder.

2. Observe the Library.

   ☐ from the upper right of the Captivate window, click **Library**

   Notice that there are images in the Library representing James as sad, happy, and confused.

3. Create a New State.

   ☐ on the Filmstrip, select slide **2** and, on the slide, select James' head

   ☐ on the **Properties Inspector**, click the **State View** button

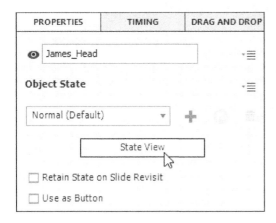

   ☐ at the left of the window, click **New State**

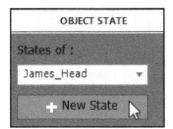

☐ change the name of the new state to **Happy**

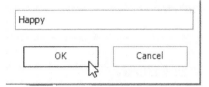

☐ click the **OK** button

4. Change the object used in a State.

☐ on the **Properties** Inspector, **Style** tab, click the button containing the words **James_RegularHead**

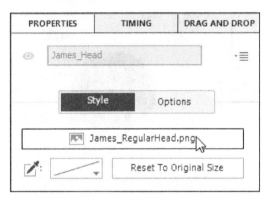

The **Select Image from Library** dialog box opens.

☐ from the list at the right, select **James_HappyHead**

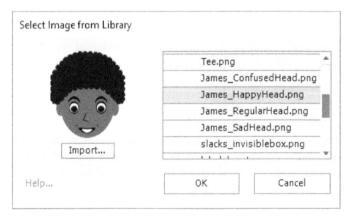

☐ click the **OK** button

5. Resize the image.

☐ with the image selected, click the **Options** tab on the **Properties Inspector**

☐ from the **Transform** area, change the **W** (width) to **144** and the **H** (height) to **148**

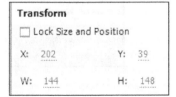

Advanced States Confidence Check

1. On the slide, ensure that James' head is still selected.

2. Create a New State named **Sad**.

3. Replace the image with **James_SadHead**.

4. Change the Width of the image to **144** and the Height to **148**.

5. Leave the State Editor by clicking **Exit State**.

6. Still working on slide **2**, from the **Drag and Drop** Inspector select the **Actions** tab.

7. From the drop-down menu in the **On Success** area, choose **Change State of**.

8. Ensure the next drop-down menu has **James_Head** selected.

9. From the next drop-down menu, choose **Happy**.

10. Ensure **Continue Playing the project** is selected.

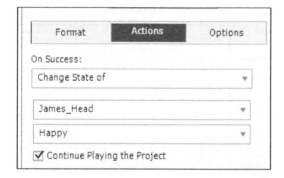

11. From the first drop-down menu in the **On Failure** area, choose **Change State of**.

12. Ensure the next drop-down menu has **James_Head** selected.

13. From the next drop-down menu, choose **Sad**.

14. Ensure **Continue Playing the project** is selected.

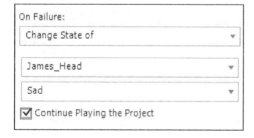

15. Preview the project.

NOTES

16. If you drag the incorrect clothing to James and click the **How do I look** button, you should see James' expression change from **Happy** to **Sad**.

17. Close the preview.

18. On the slide, ensure that James' head is still selected.

19. Add another **New State** named **Confused**.

20. Replace the existing image with **James_ConfusedHead**.

21. Change the Width of the image to **144** and the Height to **148**.

22. Exit State View.

23. For the **shirt** Drop Zone, use the Object Actions button to change the state of James' head for picking the **collared shirt** to **Happy**. (Hint: Visit the **Drag and Drop Inspector** > **Format** tab)

24. Deselect **Continue Playing Project**.

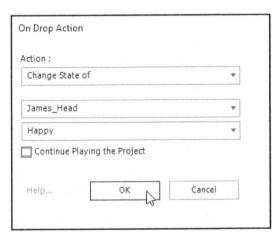

Note: You deselected **Continue Playing Project** in the step above. During the past few activities, you've been instructed to sometimes leave the option on, and at other times you've deselected it. In the step above, deselecting the option allows James' expression to change *and* prevents the Drag and Drop interaction from telling the project to continue. If you had left **Continue Playing Project** enabled, the interaction would complete and learners would not be able to interact with the **How Do I Look** button.

25. For the **shirt** Drop Zone, use the **Object Actions** button to change the **Action** if the **beer tee** is selected to display James' **Confused** face. (Don't forget to deselect **Continue Playing Project**.)

26. For the **pants** Drop Zone, use the **Object Actions** button to change the state of James' head for picking the shorts to **Confused**. (Deselect **Continue Playing Project**.)

27. For the **pants** Drop Zone, use the **Object Actions** button to change the state of James' head for picking the pants to **Happy**. (Don't forget to deselect **Continue Playing Project**.)

✔	slacks	Change State of
✔	shorts	Change State of

28. For the **shoes** Drop Zone, use the **Object Actions** button to change the state of James' head for picking the sandals to **Confused**. (Deselect **Continue Playing Project**.)

29. For the **shoes** Drop Zone, use the **Object Actions** button to change the state of James' head for picking the oxfords to **Happy**. (Deselect **Continue Playing Project**.)

	Drag Source Type	Action
✔	oxfords	Change State of
✔	sandals	Change State of

30. Preview the project and test the interaction.

31. Close the preview.

32. Save and close the project.

Drag and Drop Assets

During this module, you learned how to create a drag and drop interaction using simple shapes, and you've learned how to create more complex drag and drops that combine images and states. Now what? Where can you get cool drag and drop lessons without having to create them yourself, hiring a designer, or purchasing them on the web? You'll be happy to know that Captivate comes with a rich assortment of free Assets that include Characters, Icons, 360 images, and perhaps best of all, fully baked projects and slides that include all manner of drag and drop interactivity.

Guided Activity 35: Insert an Interactive Asset Slide

1. Create a new, blank project.

2. Access Captivate's slide Assets.

   ❏ from the upper right of the Captivate window, click **Assets**

3. Insert an Interactive slide.

   ❏ from the left of the Assets window, click **Projects**

   ❏ from beneath the **Search** area, click **Slides**

   ❏ to the right of **Slides**, click **Interactions**

   ❏ from the **Drag and Drop** column, select the **Rhapsody** interaction

   ❏ click the **Insert (1)** Slide button

   A second, fully interactive, slide is added to the project.

4. Preview the project and interact with the second slide.

   You can easily swap out the content with your own text and images. The coolest thing about the free Assets is that all of the heavy lifting has been done for you. The Drag and Drop interactions work, and the States have already been set up... it's all done. All you need to do is add the context and the content.

5. Close the preview, and then close the project (there is no need to save it).

iCONLOGiC

"Skills and Drills" Learning

Module 6: Accessible eLearning

In This Module You Will Learn About:

And You Will Learn To:

Accessibility and Captivate

You can use Captivate to create eLearning lessons that are accessible to users who have visual, hearing, mobility, or other types of disabilities.

The World Wide Web Consortium (W3C) publishes the Web Content Accessibility Guidelines, a document that specifies what designers should do to their web content to make it accessible. Many countries, including the United States, Australia, Canada, Japan, and countries in Europe, have adopted accessibility standards based on those developed by the W3C.

In the United States, the law that governs accessibility is commonly known as Section 508. Part of the Rehabilitation Act of 1973, Section 508 requires that federal agencies and federally funded organizations, such as colleges and universities, develop or use information technology that is accessible to people with disabilities.

Generally speaking, eLearning is considered accessible if it can be accessed and used by a learner who does not have to rely on a single sense or ability. Learners should be able to move through lessons using only a keyboard *or* a mouse. In addition, your lessons should include visual and auditory elements to support both hearing and visually impaired users.

One of the easiest things you can do to make your Captivate projects accessible is to select Enable Accessibility within an open project (Windows users, **Edit > Preferences > Project > Publish Settings**; Mac users, **Adobe Captivate > Preferences > Project > Publish Settings**). Combining this selection with filling in the Project name and Description (**File > Project Info**) allows an assistive device to read the name and description aloud when a learner accesses the lesson.

The following Captivate elements are accessible when Enable Accessibility is selected:

- ☐ Project name
- ☐ Project description
- ☐ Slide accessibility text
- ☐ Slide names
- ☐ Text buttons
- ☐ Playback controls (The function of each button is read by screen readers.)
- ☐ Password protection (When a Captivate SWF file is password protected, the prompt for a password is read by screen readers.)
- ☐ Question slides (Some Question slides are not considered accessible. Multiple choice and true/false are the easiest ones for a visually impaired learner to navigate.)

For more information on creating and viewing accessible content using Adobe products, visit **http://blogs.adobe.com/accessibility/**. You can learn more about Section 508 by visiting **www.section508.gov**.

Guided Activity 36: Set Document Information

1. Open **ComplyMe** from the Captivate2019BeyondData folder.

2. Add Document Information that will be read by a screen reader.

   ❏ choose **File > Project Info**

   The Preferences dialog box appears.

   ❏ in the **Author** field, type **Biff Bifferson**

   ❏ in the **Company** field, type **Super Simplistic Solutions**

   ❏ in the **E-mail** field, type **biff.bifferson@supersimplisticsolutions.com**

   ❏ in the **Website** field, type **www.supersimplisticsolutions.com**

   ❏ in the **Copyright** field, type **Super Simplistic Solutions. All rights reserved.**

   ❏ in the **Project Name** field, type **Creating New Folders: An Interactive Simulation**

   ❏ in the **Description** field, type **This simulation will teach you how to create new folders on your computer.**

Project: Information	
Author:	Biff Bifferson
Company:	Super Simplistic Solutions
E-mail:	biff.bifferson@supersimplisticsolutions.com
Website:	www.supersimplisticsolutions.com
Copyright:	Super Simplistic Solutions. All rights reserved.
Project Name:	Creating New Folders: An Interactive Simulation
Description:	This simulation will teach you how to create new folders on your computer.

   Keep in mind that although you filled in several of the Project Information fields, only the Project Name and Description you typed are useful for compliance. This text is typically read aloud by an assistive device when the lesson is first opened by the learner.

3. Leave the Preferences dialog box open for the next activity.

Guided Activity 37: Enable Accessibility

1. Ensure that the **ComplyMe** project is still open and the **Preferences** dialog box is still open.

2. Enable Accessibility for the project.

   ❏ from the **Project** category, select **Publish Settings**

   ❏ select **Enable Accessibility** to turn the option on

   Project: Publish Settings

   Frames Per Second: 30

   ☑ Publish Adobe Connect metadata.

   ☑ Include Mouse

   ☑ Enable Accessibility

   ☐ Restrict keyboard tabbing to slide items only

   ☐ Hide selection rectangle for slide items in HTML5

   ☑ Include Audio

   ☑ Publish Audio as Mono

   ☑ Play tap audio for recorded typing

   Externalize Resources: ☐ Skin

   ☐ Widgets

   ☐ FMR SWF

   ☐ Animations

By selecting Enable Accessibility, you have enabled your published lessons to be viewed by devices, browsers, and assistive software that support accessibility.

Note: Enable Accessibility is on by default in all Captivate projects, and there is little reason to ever disable it. I disabled the feature in this project for training purposes only.

   ❏ click the **OK** button

3. Save your work.

Accessibility Text

According to Axistive (**http://www.axistive.com**), the three main screen readers in North America are (in order of market share) **JAWS**, **Window-Eyes**, and **Hal**, which together sell around 3,000 (units) yearly.

Generally speaking, the text that will be read by the screen reader includes the Project Name (first) and Description (second) that you set up earlier. (See "Set Document Information" on page 107.) The next thing that an assistive device reads is the slide's accessibility text and then any accessibility text added to slide objects.

Guided Activity 38: Add Accessibility Text to Slides

1. Ensure that the **ComplyMe** project is still open.

2. Add Slide Accessibility text to a slide.

    ☐ on the **Filmstrip**, select slide **1**

    Screen readers will not "see" slide backgrounds. When a visually impaired learner accesses this slide, the assistive device reads the Slide Accessibility text aloud. You can either type the accessibility text or, if the text is part of the Slide Notes, import them from the Notes area.

    ☐ on the **Properties Inspector**, click the menu in the top right and choose **Accessibility**

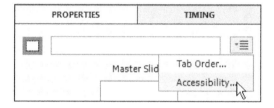

    The Slide Accessibility dialog box opens.

    ☐ click the **Import Slide Notes** button

    ☐ from the bottom of the imported text, delete the last sentence "Click to add notes for the selected slide"

    ☐ click the **OK** button

3. Name a slide.

❏ on the **Properties Inspector**, click within the **Name** field

❏ type **Begin Lesson** and then press **[enter]** on your keyboard

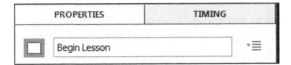

The name appears both in the Name field and beneath the slide on the Filmstrip. This text is also read aloud by assistive devices.

4. Save your work.

Guided Activity 39: Import Slide Audio

1. Ensure that the **ComplyMe** project is still open.

2. Add Audio to slide 1.

   ☐ on the Filmstrip, right-click slide **1** and choose **Audio > Import**

   ☐ navigate to **Captivate2019BeyondData > audio**

   ☐ open **comply_slide1.wav**

   Audio is added to the slide (you can confirm this via the speaker icon visible on the slide's Filmstrip thumbnail).

Are you wondering why you added audio to a slide that already includes Accessibility Text? The audio is for the benefit of learners who are *not* visually disabled. Many people assume that a project is compliant if it includes Accessibility Text *or* slide audio, and if both exist, they will be in direct conflict with each other. In my experience, learners who are visually impaired typically rely solely on the screen reader and ignore (or even mute) the slide audio. I've been told by more than one visually impaired learner that the slide audio is annoying, often sounding like the narrator is speaking too slowly.

Accessibility Text Confidence Check

1. Select slide **2** on the Filmstrip and, from the top right of the **Properties Inspector**, click the menu and choose **Accessibility**.

2. Add the following Accessibility text: **During this interactive lesson you will have a chance to create a new folder. New folders can be created in any window. While you can give a folder any name up to 255 characters, it's a good idea to keep the character count smaller rather than larger.**

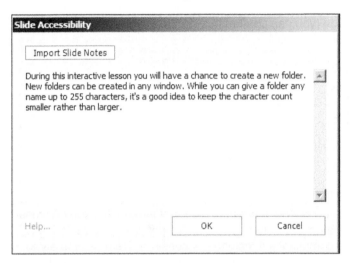

3. Name slide 2 **Lesson Overview**.

4. Add the following audio to slide **2**: **comply_slide2.wav**.

5. When the Audio Import Options dialog box appears, select the first option (to show the slide for that same amount of time as the length of the audio). If you see this dialog box throughout this Confidence Check, always choose the first option.

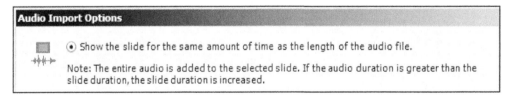

6. Go to slide **3** and add the following Accessibility text to the slide: **To create a new folder, first select the File menu.**

7. Name the slide **Select File menu**.

8. Add the following audio to slide **3**: **comply_slide3.wav**.

9. Go to slide **5** and add the following Accessibility text to the slide: **Now select the New menu item.**

10. Name the slide **Select New Command**.

11. Add the following audio to slide **5**: **comply_slide5.wav**.

12. Go to slide **6** and add the following Accessibility text to the slide: **The final step is to select the Folder menu item. Go ahead and do that now.**

13. Name the slide **Select Folder Command**.

14. Add the following audio to slide **6**: **comply_slide6.wav**.

15. Go to slide **8** and add the following Accessibility text to the slide: **And there's your new folder. Go ahead and select the new folder to end this lesson.**

16. Name the slide **Select the New Folder**.

17. Add the following audio to slide **8**: **comply_slide8.wav**.

18. Preview the project.

    There should be audio on the appropriate slides. However, none of the buttons on the slides are *keyboard accessible.* Learners should be able to press a key on the keyboard to move from slide to slide. You will fix this problem next.

19. Close the preview.

20. Save and close the project.

NOTES

Shortcut Keys

You can attach a keyboard shortcut to any interactive object in Captivate (interactive objects include buttons, click boxes, text entry boxes, etc.). Not only are shortcut keys an important component of accessibility, many learners who are able to use a mouse to click objects elect to use shortcut keys as an alternative to using the mouse.

> **Note:** Although you can use just about any keyboard shortcut or combination of keys as your shortcut keys, you should carefully test those shortcuts in several web browsers. Some keyboard shortcuts are reserved by the browser. The keys might work as expected when you preview the lesson from within Captivate. However, when you preview the lesson in a browser, the keys might be intercepted by the web browser and not work as expected. (For instance, the [**F1**] key historically displays the browser's Help window.)

Guided Activity 40: Add Shortcut Keys

1. Open **ShortcutCCMe** from the Captivate2019BeyondData folder.

2. Attach a shortcut key to a button.

   ❑ on slide **1**, double-click the **Continue** button

   ❑ on the **Properties Inspector**, select the **Actions** tab

   ❑ just beneath **Shortcut**, click the radio button

   ❑ on your keyboard, press [**enter**] (PC) or [**return**] (Mac)

   The shortcut appears in the Shortcut field.

3. Attach a shortcut key to the button on slide 2.

   ❑ go to slide **2**

   ❑ select the **Continue** button

   ❑ on the **Properties Inspector**, select the **Actions** tab

   ❑ just beneath **Shortcut**, click the radio button

   ❑ on your keyboard, press [**enter**] (PC) or [**return**] (Mac)

4. Attach a multi-key shortcut to a click box.

☐ go to slide **3**

☐ on the **Timeline**, select the **Click Box**

☐ on the **Properties Inspector**, select the **Actions** tab

☐ just beneath **Shortcut**, click the radio button

☐ on your keyboard, press [**alt**] [**f**] (Mac users, press [**option**] [**f**])

Captivate on the PC shown above; Captivate for the Mac shown at the right.

5. Test the shortcut keys.

☐ select slide **1**

☐ choose **Preview > Next 5 Slides**

☐ when the first slide appears, press [**enter**] or [**return**] to go to the next slide

☐ when the second slide appears, press [**enter**] or [**return**] to go to the next slide

☐ when the third slide appears, Windows users press [**alt**] [**f**] (Mac users press [**option**] [**f**]) to go to the next slide

The keys should have worked as expected. Let's see what happens when you preview the lesson through a web browser.

6. Close the preview.

7. Preview via a web browser.

☐ choose **Preview > HTML5 in Browser**

☐ after the lesson begins, press [**enter**] or [**return**] to move through the first two slides

☐ when the third slide appears, press [**alt**] [**f**] ([**option**] [**f**] on a Mac) to go to the next slide

If you are using a Windows-based browser, the [**alt**] [**f**] combination probably worked, and you advanced to the next slide. (I noticed that the combination did not work in Microsoft Edge.) However, the [**alt**] [**f**] combination also opened the File menu in the browser. If you are a Mac user running Safari, the [**option**] [**f**] combination isn't supported. Because you cannot stop keys from activating web browser functions or always predict how some key combinations work in every web browser, it's best to shy away from key combinations and use single-key shortcuts.

NOTES

8. Close the browser window and return to the Captivate project.

9. Edit assigned shortcut keys.

□ go to slide **3** and, on the **Timeline**, select the **Click Box**

□ on the **Properties Inspector**, click in the **Shortcut** field

□ press **[f]** on your keyboard

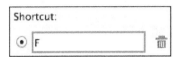

10. Preview the project as **HTML5 in Browser** and ensure that the shortcut keys work as expected.

11. Close the browser and return to the Captivate project.

Keyboard Shortcut Confidence Check

1. Still working in the **Shortcut_CCMe** project, go to slide **5** and attach the following letter shortcut to the click box: **N**.

2. Go to slide **6** and attach the following letter shortcut to the click box: **F**.

3. Go to slide **8** and attach the following letter shortcut to the click box: **F**.

4. Preview the project as **HTML5 in Browser** and ensure that the shortcut keys work as expected.

5. When finished, close the browser window and return to the Captivate project.

6. On slide **1**, open the slide's **Accessibility** dialog box (you learned how to add slide Accessibility on page 109).

7. Add the following text after the word "button": **(or press ENTER on your keyboard)**.

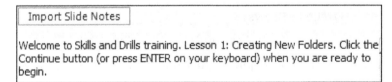

8. Continue through the rest of the slides, adding Accessibility Text as necessary so that screen readers alert a learner as to which shortcut key to press when a slide with interactivity is accessed.

9. When finished, save your work.

Closed Captioning

Closed captioning allows you to provide descriptive information that explains the audio recording in written text. If your playbar contains a CC button (most playbars do by default), a learner has the option to click the CC button, which displays a panel where the closed caption text appears.

Guided Activity 41: Add Closed Captions

1. Ensure that the **Shortcut_CCMe** project is still open.

2. Show the Advanced Audio Management dialog box.

   ❏ choose **Audio > Audio Management**

   Six of the slides contain audio clips. (Notice that the Sound column for those slides contains the word "Yes.") You can add Closed Captions only to slides containing slide-level audio.

Slide/Object	Sound	Durations
Begin Lesson	Yes	00:00:07.800
Lesson Overview	Yes	00:00:15.300
Select File menu	Yes	00:00:03.700
Slide4	No	
Select New Co...	Yes	00:00:03.0
Select Folder C...	Yes	00:00:05.300
Slide7	No	
Select the New ...	Yes	00:00:05.100
Slide9	No	

3. Add Closed Captions to a slide.

   ❏ from the **Slide/Object** column, select **Begin Lesson**

   This is one of the six slides that has audio and therefore can be captioned.

   ❏ at the bottom of the dialog box, click the **Closed Caption** tool

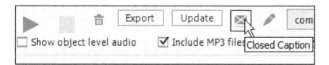

The Slide Audio dialog box opens, and the Closed Captioning tab is selected. You can add closed captions anywhere on the waveform. To begin, you'll be adding a closed caption at the beginning. But first, let's zoom away from the waveform a bit so you can see more of it.

   ❏ drag the zoom slider **left** to around **19** or **20**

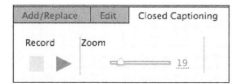

By zooming away from the waveform, you can see the entire wave. Notice that the waveform has three segments. Each of the segments will be marked as captions.

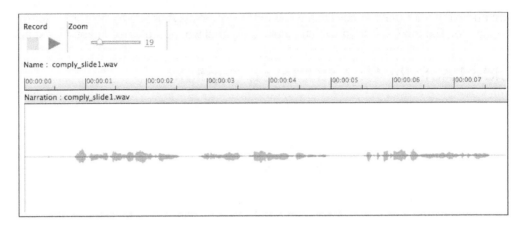

❏ click just in front of the first segment on the waveform

❏ at the right of the dialog box, click the **Add Closed Caption** tool

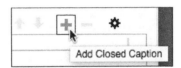

❏ in the Caption area, replace the placeholder text with **Welcome to skills and drills training.**

The caption text appears in Row 1, and there is an orange caption mark and the number "1" on the waveform.

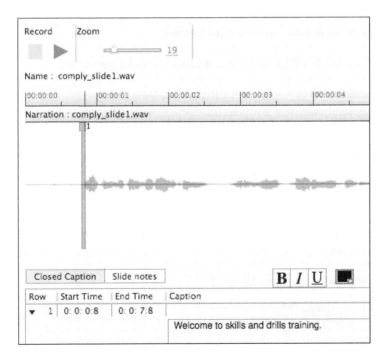

4. Add a second Closed Caption to the slide.

☐ on the waveform, click just in front of the second segment (just before the 3 second mark)

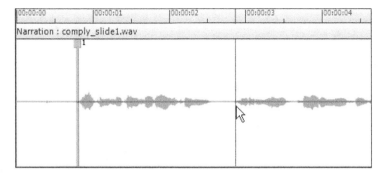

☐ click the **Add Closed Caption** tool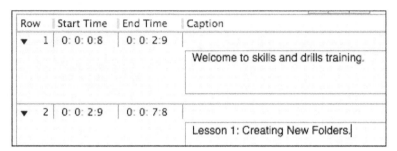

☐ in the Caption area, replace the placeholder text with **Lesson 1: Creating New Folders.**

Row	Start Time	End Time	Caption
▼ 1	0: 0: 0:8	0: 0: 2:9	
			Welcome to skills and drills training.
▼ 2	0: 0: 2:9	0: 0: 7:8	
			Lesson 1: Creating New Folders.

5. Add a third Closed Caption to the slide.

☐ on the waveform, click just in front of the third segment (just before the 5.5 second mark)

☐ click the **Add Closed Caption** tool

☐ in the Caption area, type **Click the Continue button when you are ready to begin.**

▼ 3	0: 0: 5:5	0: 0: 7:8	
			Click the Continue button when you are ready to begin.

NOTES

Your three closed captions should look similar to the image below.

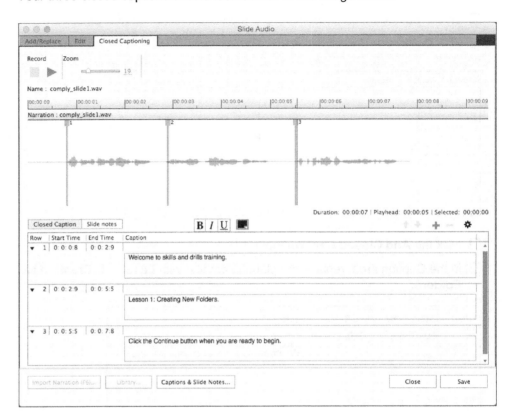

☐ click the **Save** button

☐ click the **Close** button (to close the Slide Audio dialog box)

☐ click the **OK** button (to close the Advanced Audio Management dialog box)

6. Save your work.

Closed Captions Confidence Check

1. Preview the first five slides. As soon as slide **1** appears, click the **CC** button on the playbar to see the Closed Captions you added during the last activity.

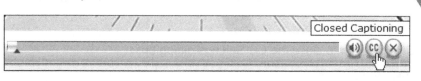

Notice that the Closed Captions are synchronized to match the audio, sentence by sentence. However, the Closed Caption text is a bit hard to read and too narrow. You will fix those problems next.

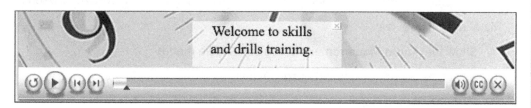

2. Close the preview.

3. Show the Skin Editor (**Project > Skin Editor**).

4. At the lower left of the dialog box, below the **Closed Captioning** check box, click the **Settings** button to display the **CC Settings** dialog box.

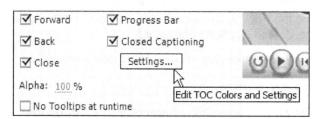

5. From the center of the dialog box, click the first drop-down menu and choose **Project**.

6. From the left of the dialog box, select **Show Closed Captions**.

7. From the **Font** drop-down menu area, change the Font to **Verdana**

8. Change the Size to **15**.

9. From the **Align** drop-down menu, choose **Bottom Center**.

10. Change the **W** to **75%** and the **H** to **10%**. (The width of your closed captions will now take up 75% of the lesson's screen area and 10% of the height.)

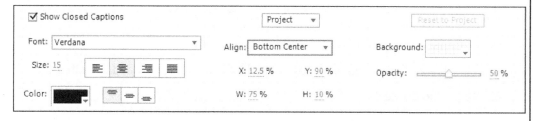

11. From the bottom left of the dialog box, select **Override Slide Level Settings with Project Settings**.

    Any manual Closed Caption settings made slide by slide are removed and the closed captions formatted consistently throughout the project. However, it's good to know that the appearance and position of the closed captions can be unique from slide by slide.

12. Click the **Apply** button.

13. Click the **Close** button to close the CC Settings dialog box.

14. Close the Skin Editor window.

15. Preview the first five slides of the project again. This time, the closed captions automatically appear (thanks to the **Show Closed Captions** option you selected in the CC Settings dialog box. In addition, the formatting of the closed captions matches your new custom settings (the font, font size, and size of the caption area have been modified).

16. Close the preview.

17. Show the **Audio Management** dialog box (Audio menu).

18. Select the audio for slide **2** (Lesson Overview).

19. Click the Closed Caption tool.

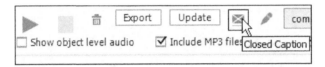

20. Add three Closed Captions in front of the main segments along the waveform. (Consider listening to the audio by clicking the Play button prior to adding the Closed Captions. Doing so helps you position the Closed Captions correctly.)

    During this interactive lesson you will have a chance to create a new folder.

    New folders can be created in any window.

    While you can give a folder any name up to 255 characters, it's a good idea to keep the character count smaller rather than larger.

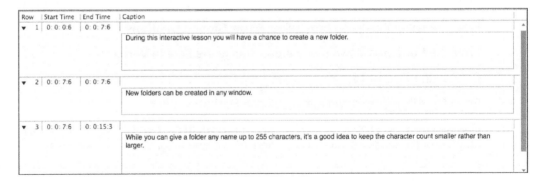

21. Preview the project from slide **1** and review the Closed Captions.

22. On slide 2, there is too much text in the last caption. You'll need to fix that.

23. Close the preview.

24. Open the **Audio Management** dialog box, select the **second** slide, and click the **Closed Caption** tool.

25. Select the **second half** of the text in the last caption and then **cut** it to the clipboard.

26. Add a new closed caption on the waveform (where the narrator is saying aloud the text you just cut) and **paste** the text on the clipboard into the closed caption text area.

    As you've probably guessed, Closed Captions aren't difficult to add to your project but can add a significant amount of labor to your production load. Here's a little nugget that might speed things along.

27. Go to slide **3**.

28. Choose **Window > Slide Notes** to open the Slide Notes panel.

29. Click in the Slide Notes panel at the bottom of your window where it says **Click to add notes for the selected slide**.

30. Replace the placeholder text with **To create a new folder, first select the File menu.**

31. At the top right of the Slide Notes panel, select the **Audio CC** check box.

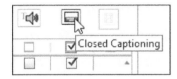

32. Click the **Closed Captioning** icon.

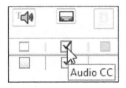

33. On the Closed Captioning tab, notice that the Closed Caption has already been added to the waveform. You can drag the closed caption mark to the right to better synchronize the Closed Caption with the audio.

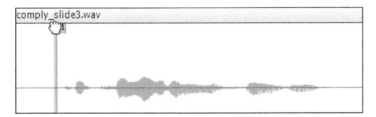

34. Proceed through the rest of the project and add Closed Captions as necessary.

35. When finished adding the Closed Captions to the project, preview the entire project and ensure that the Closed Captions are synched with the audio.

36. When finished, close the Preview.

37. Save your work and close the project.

Tab Order

Learners have always been able to select screen objects on published Captivate lessons by either clicking the mouse or using the [**tab**] key on the keyboard. However, your ability to control which screen objects came into focus when the learner pressed the [**tab**] key *was* beyond your control. I emphasize the word *was*... thanks to Captivate's Tab Order controls, you can now determine which interactive screen objects come into focus when the learner presses the [**tab**] key. As a bonus, the Tab Order you establish also controls when the Accessibility text added to interactive objects is read aloud by a screen reader.

Guided Activity 42: Set a Tab Order

1. Open **TabOrderMe** from the Captivate2019BeyondData folder.

    This is a simple, single-slide project containing three interactive buttons. The buttons have been set up to play a sound when clicked.

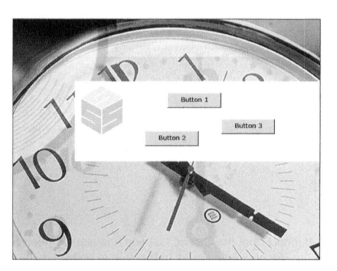

2. Preview the project.

3. Press the [**tab**] key on your keyboard.

    As you press the [**tab**] key, notice that you move around the slide and select each button in a logical order (Button 1, Button 2, and Button 3). After tabbing past Button 3, you are taken around the tools on the playbar and then back to Button 1.

    When learners press the [**tab**] key, you want to forgo logical navigation and have Button 2 be the first button selected, then Button 3, and finally Button 1. You'll set that up next using Captivate's Tab Order feature.

4. Close the Preview.

5. Set a Tab Order.

☐ expand the Timeline

Notice the stacking order of the slide objects. Button1, named **First_Button**, is on the bottom of the stack.

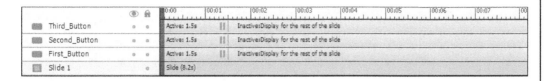

☐ on the Timeline, drag **First_Button** to the top of the object stack

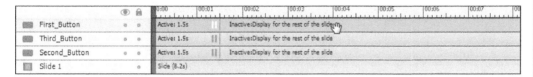

6. Preview the project and press the **[tab]** key on your keyboard to navigate around the slide.

As you press the **[tab]** key, you should select Button 2 first, Button 3 second, and Button 1 third.

7. Close the preview.

8. Save your work.

9. Close the project.

Notes

iCONLOGiC

"Skills and Drills" Learning

Module 7: Advanced Actions

In This Module You Will Learn About:

And You Will Learn To:

Standard Actions

If you want an interactive object (Button, Click Box, or Text Entry Box) to perform a single Action, it's a simple matter of selecting the object and visiting the Actions tab on the Properties Inspector. Common actions include jumping to a slide, playing a sound, or even opening a website or a file.

During the lessons that follow, you will create an interactive recipe that teaches a learner how to make Biff's famous caramel apples. Along the way you will use standard actions, conditional actions, and combo actions that provide the learner with an adjusted list of ingredients based on the number of caramel apples the learner wants to make. In addition, you'll set things up so that with a click of a button, learners are able to view images of the shopping list and the finished caramel apple.

Guided Activity 43: Use a Completed Action

1. Open **ActionMe_Complete** from the Captivate2019BeyondData folder.

   This project contains all of the actions that you will learn to create during this module.

2. Preview the project.

3. Click the **Shopping List** button.

   A picture of each ingredient needed to create a caramel apple appears.

4. Click the **Caramel Apple** button.

   The ingredients disappear and are replaced by the finished apple.

5. Click the **Directions** button to move to the next slide.

6. Type a number between 1 and 7 into the desired servings text entry box and then click the **Update Recipe** button.

   The amount of each ingredient changes to reflect the number of servings you requested.

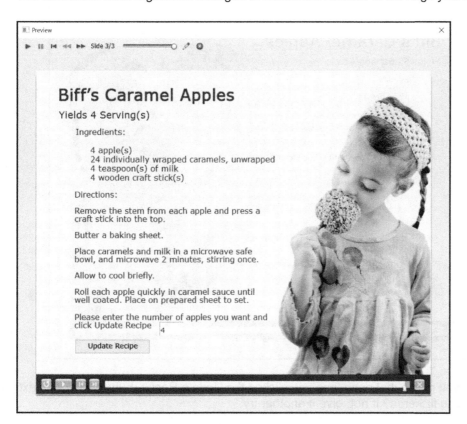

Are you curious to learn what will happen if you enter **0** for the number of apples?

7. Type a **0** into the Desired Servings text entry box and click the **Update Recipe** button.

   A caption appears indicating that using a value of 0 was not a good idea.

> Huh? Are you on a diet?
> Please enter a value greater than 0.

What if you need more than seven apples?

---

8. Enter a number larger than 7 for the desired servings and click the **Update Recipe** button.

A tip is displayed at the right warning you about trying to melt too much caramel at a time.

Did you notice that each time you clicked the Update Recipe button the Yield text below the title flickered? If not, give it another try.

Now that you know what the recipe project looks like and how it should behave, you can get down to adding the actions required to make everything work.

9. Close the preview.

10. Close the project without saving.

Guided Activity 44: Name Objects

1. Open **StandardActionMe** from the Captivate2019BeyondData folder.

2. Name slide objects.

   ☐ go to slide **2**

   With all of the images stacked on top of one another, the slide is a mess—but it's organized chaos. When the learner gets to this slide, most of the images will be hidden. Specific images will appear or disappear as the appropriate slide buttons are clicked.

   ☐ on the slide, double-click the image of the **green apple**

   On the Properties Inspector, notice that the apple image has a nondescript name (Image_2). You will soon need to locate some of the images within a drop-down menu in the Advanced Actions dialog box. Naming an object makes that task easier.

   ☐ from the top of the Properties Inspector, change **Name** to **Apple**

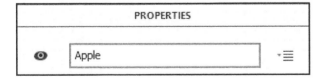

   At the far left of the Timeline, notice that the new name for the apple appears.

Naming Objects Confidence Check

1. Give the remaining images names as follows:

   Image of popsicle sticks: **Sticks**

   Image of caramels: **Caramels**

   Image of quart of milk: **Milk**

   Image of finished caramel apple: **CaramelApple**

		👁	🔒	00:00	00:01	00:02	00:03	00:04
🖼	Sticks	●	●	sticks:Display for the rest of the slide				END
🖼	Milk	●	●	milk:Display for the rest of the slide				
🖼	Caramels	●	●	caramel:Display for the rest of the slide				
🖼	CaramelApple	●	●	Apple_Nuts:Display for the rest of the slide				
🖼	Apple	●	●	greenApple_T:Display for the rest of the slide				

2. Save your work.

   Note: You've spent a fair amount of time naming objects. I bet you're wondering if there's any real value to the endeavor. As you begin creating advanced actions and need to select objects from a drop-down menu containing dozens of objects, you will find that naming slides and slide objects pays huge dividends.

Guided Activity 45: Create a Mask

1. Ensure that the **StandardActionMe** project is still open.

2. Use a Highlight Box as a mask.

   ☐ ensure that you are still on slide **2**

   ☐ choose **View > Magnification > 50%**

   There is a large Highlight Box on the **Scrap Area** at the right.

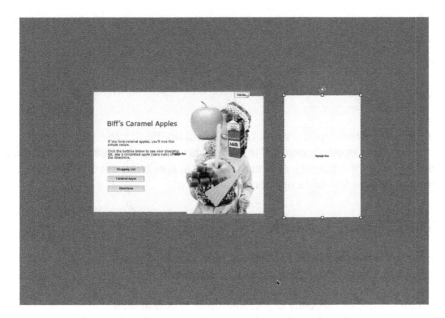

Because Scrap Area objects neither Preview nor Publish, the Scrap Area is a great place to drop objects while you try to determine how or where you are going to use them.

☐ drag the Highlight Box onto the slide so that it covers the image of the little girl (you will use Actions in just a bit to make the Highlight Box hide the girl on the slide when the learner clicks a button)

Notice that after you drag the Highlight Box (it has the name **GirlMask**) onto the picture of the girl, it automatically covers the girl but goes behind the other slide objects. This is caused by the vertical stacking order of the slide objects on the Timeline.

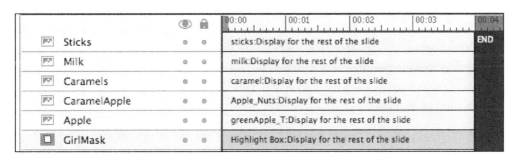

Guided Activity 46: Control Object Visibility

1. Ensure that the **StandardActionMe** project is still open.

   When you previewed the completed project (ActionMe_Complete), you might recall that the ingredients did not appear until after you clicked a button. The reason is simple enough: the **Visible in output** option.

2. Make the Apple image invisible in the output.

   ☐ select the **Apple** image

   ☐ on the **Properties** Inspector, to the left of the **Name** field, click **Visible in output**

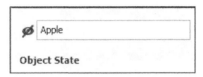

   Clicking **Visible in output** appears to have no effect on the Apple—you can still see it on the slide. The visibility option controls if the object is visible to the learner in the *published* version of the lesson (the output). Although the Apple has been set to initially be invisible to the learner, it can be forced to appear via an Action.

Visibility Confidence Check

1. Select each of the remaining images (Sticks, Milk, Caramels, CaramelApple) and make them **Not Visible in output**.

   Note: You can control the visibility of multiple objects at one time. Select multiple objects by using [shift]-click and then click **Visible in output**.

2. Save your work.

Guided Activity 47: Create a Standard Advanced Action

1. Ensure that the **StandardActionMe** project is still open.

   If you want to make a single hidden image appear, that's easy. Select a button and, from the Actions tab of the Properties Inspector, choose **Show** from the **On Success** drop-down menu. Lastly, select an image from the **Show** drop-down menu.

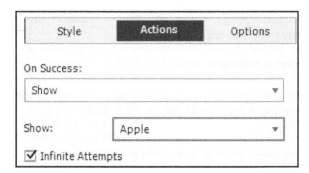

   Your goal is to display *all* of the images that make up the ingredients at one time. To perform that bit of wizardry, you need to create an Advanced Action. It will be a simple **Advanced Action**, but an Advanced Action nevertheless.

2. Open the Advanced Actions dialog box.

   ☐ still working on slide **2**, choose **Project > Advanced Actions**

   The Advanced Actions dialog box opens.

3. Create an Action.

   ☐ in the **Action Name** field, type **displayShoppingList**

   ☐ in the **Actions** area, double-click the **first row**

   ☐ from the **Select Action** drop-down menu, choose **Show**

   Note: The items in the menu **are not listed alphabetically**. You will need to scroll down the list to find **Show**.

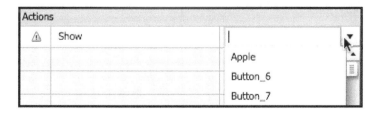

   Notice that there is a yellow warning icon to the left of the Action. This is a visual indicator that the Action is not complete.

NOTES

When you selected Show, a drop-down menu opened to the right. All of the objects in the project are represented in this list. Some of the objects have default item names assigned by Captivate (such as Text_Caption_11). It's a good bet that you don't know which caption is number 11. Thanks to the names you assigned the images a moment ago, you can see those objects by name in the menu. It is not necessary to name every object in a project. However, if you need to locate an object within a drop-down list (like now), giving it a unique and meaningful name is important.

You need to cover up the image of the little girl. You will do this by "showing" the Highlight Box (the Highlight Box has already been named **GirlMask**).

❑ from the drop-down menu, choose **GirlMask**

Notice that the warning sign at the left is now a green checkmark. The green checkmark indicates that the Action row is complete. Of course, the Action might be wrong, but at least the syntax is correct and complete.

Actions		
✔	Show	GirlMask

❑ double-click in the **next row** in the **Actions** area

❑ from the **Select Action** drop-down menu, choose **Show**

Once again, notice the warning sign indicating that the Action is not yet complete.

❑ from the drop-down menu, choose **Apple**

The yellow warning sign turns into a green checkmark indicating that the Action row is complete.

Standard Action Confidence Check

1. Add more rows to the Action that will show the Caramels, Milk, and Sticks.

   Ensure that all of the rows are green (indicating that each of the Action rows is complete).

Actions		
✅	Show	GirlMask
✅	Show	Apple
✅	Show	Caramels
✅	Show	Milk
✅	Show	Sticks

2. Click the **Save As Action** button and then click the **OK** button when notified of the successful save.

   One small piece of the action is missing. In the completed lesson, clicking the **Shopping List** button not only displayed all four ingredients but also hid the picture of the final product (the Caramel Apple). You need to insert one more line into the action for this to work.

3. Double-click the next available blank row and from the **Select Action** drop-down menu, choose **Hide**.

4. From the drop-down menu, choose **CaramelApple**.

5. Click the **Update Action** button and then click the **OK** button.

   Your Action should look like this:

Actions		
✅	Show	GirlMask
✅	Show	Apple
✅	Show	Caramels
✅	Show	Milk
✅	Show	Sticks
✅	Hide	CaramelApple

Note: Curious about what to do if you enter an erroneous Action line and need to remove it? Or perhaps you'd like to duplicate a line and save yourself some repetitive work? You'll find standard Cut, Copy, Paste, and Remove tools in the upper right of the Actions area in the dialog box. You will use some of these tools soon.

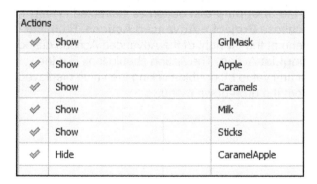

6. Click the **Close** button to close the Advanced Actions dialog box.

7. Save the project.

Guided Activity 48: Execute an Advanced Action

1. Ensure that the **StandardActionMe** project is still open.

   You have created an Advanced Action, but there is nothing in the project that is making the Action kick into, well, action. Next you will attach the Advanced Action to the **Shopping List** button on slide **2**.

   When a learner clicks the button, the Action "kicks in."

   ☐ on slide **2**, select the **Shopping List button**

   ☐ on the **Properties Inspector**, select the **Actions** tab

   ☐ from the **On Success** drop-down menu, choose **Execute Advanced Actions**

   ☐ from the **Script** drop-down menu, notice that **displayShoppingList** is selected (because it's currently the project's only Advanced Action)

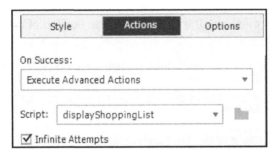

2. Preview the project and click the Shopping List button.

   The ingredients you need to purchase should appear, and the little girl should disappear.

   Note: If the Action does not work, first ensure you have attached the **displayShoppingList** Action to the **Shopping List** button as instructed in step 1 above. If that isn't the problem, choose **Project > Advanced Actions**. From the **Existing Actions** drop-down menu at the far right of the Advanced Actions dialog box, choose the **displayShoppingList** Action. The Action should look like the image below. If not, you can edit any value by double-clicking the value displayed and making a different choice from the drop-down menu.

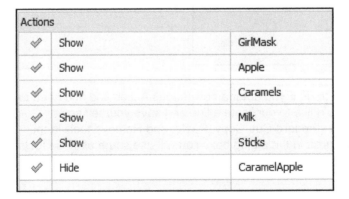

3. Close the preview, and then save and close the project.

Guided Activity 49: Group Timeline Objects

1. Open the **StandardActionMe_Step2** project from the Captivate2019BeyondData folder.

   During the last activity, did you find it tedious to have to Show each item in the shopping list one at a time as you added the Actions? Wouldn't it be nice if you could Show all of the ingredients using just one command line in the Action? If you group the Shopping List items together, it's a lot faster to build the Advanced Action.

   ☐ go to slide **2** and select all of the shopping list images (**Apple, Sticks, Milk, Caramels**)

   Note: You can select multiple objects by selecting one, pressing [**shift**] on your keyboard and then selecting the others.) Be careful not to select more of the slide objects than those mentioned above. **Only four images should be selected**.

   ☐ with the four images selected, choose **Edit > Group**

   The images are grouped not only on the slide but also on the Timeline. Because the **Visible in output** option was deselected for each of the selected items, the group is initially invisible to the learner.

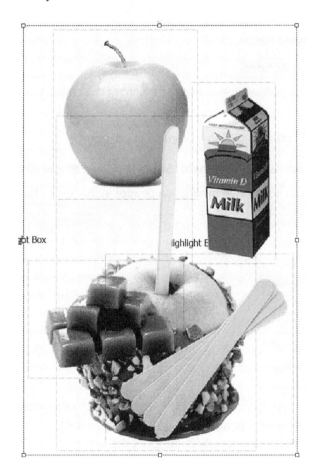

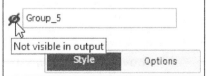

On the Timeline, the triangle to the left of the group name can be clicked to collapse or expand the group. The objects can still be manipulated individually, but they can now also work together as a group.

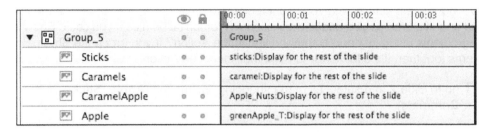

2. Name the group.

   ☐ on the Timeline, ensure that the group is selected

   ☐ on the Properties Inspector, change the group's Name to **ShoppingListGroup** and then press [**enter**]

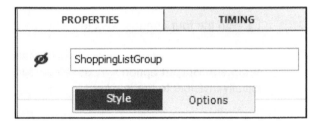

3. Remove actions from an Advanced Action.

   ☐ choose **Project > Advanced Actions**

   ☐ from the **Existing Actions** drop-down menu at the far right of the dialog box, choose **displayShoppingList**

This is the Advanced Action you created during the previous activity.

   ☐ select the following three rows: **Show Caramels**, **Show Milk**, and **Show Sticks**

   ☐ click the **Remove** icon (shown just above the mouse pointer in the image below)

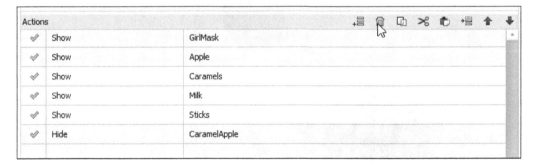

Note: There are two, nearly identical icons in the Advanced Actions dialog box: **Remove** and **Delete action**. The **Delete action** icon is in the upper right of the dialog box and will delete the entire Advanced Action. Ensure you click the **Remove** icon, which will delete the selected Action lines, not the entire Advanced Action.

4. Edit a line in the Action so that it uses the Group you created a moment ago.

☐ in the **Advanced Actions** dialog box, double-click the word **Apple**

☐ from the drop-down menu, choose **ShoppingListGroup**

Actions		
✅	Show	GirlMask
✅	Show	ShoppingListGroup
✅	Hide	CaramelApple

☐ click the **Update Action** button (and click the **OK** button when prompted)

☐ click the **Close** button to close the Advanced Actions dialog box

You need to create an Advanced Action for the **Caramel Apple** button. This Action is similar to the **Shopping List** button, but in reverse. Instead of showing all of the ingredients and then hiding the finished apple, you hide all of the ingredients and show the finished apple.

5. Duplicate an Action.

☐ working on slide **2**, select the **Caramel Apple** button (be careful to select the button, not the image)

☐ on the **Properties Inspector**, select the **Actions** tab

☐ from the **On Success** drop-down menu, choose **Execute Advanced Actions**

☐ at the right of the Script drop-down menu, click **Advanced Actions**

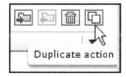

Clicking Advanced Actions is an alternate method of getting to the Advanced Actions dialog box (**Project > Advanced Actions**).

☐ from the **Existing Actions** drop-down menu, ensure **displayShoppingList** is selected

☐ from the upper right of the dialog box, click the **Duplicate action** icon

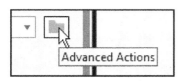

The duplicate action is named **Duplicate_Of_displayShoppingList** by default.

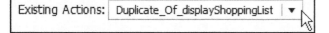

NOTES

6. Rename an Action.

❏ in the **Action Name** field, change the name of the action to **displayCaramelApple**

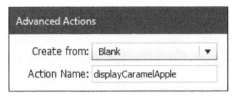

Advanced Actions

Create from: Blank ▼

Action Name: displayCaramelApple

❏ click the **Update Action** button

❏ click the **OK** button

7. Edit the new Action.

❏ to the left of the **ShoppingListGroup** Action, double-click the word **Show**

The word changes to the Select Action drop-down menu.

❏ from the **Select Action** drop-down menu, choose **Hide**

❏ from the next drop-down menu, choose **ShoppingListGroup**

| ✅ | Hide | ShoppingListGroup |

8. Update the Action.

❏ click the **Update Action** button

❏ click the **OK** button

Editing Actions Confidence Check

1. Edit the **displayCaramelApple** action to Show the **CaramelApple**.

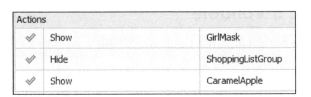

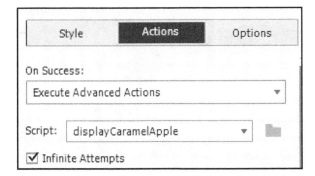

2. Update the Action.

3. Close the Advanced Actions dialog box.

4. With the **Caramel Apple** button selected on slide 2, select **displayCaramelApple** as the **Script** to Execute.

5. Peview the project.

6. During the preview, click back and forth between the **Shopping List** and **Caramel Apple** buttons.

   The images should switch back and forth on demand.

7. Close the preview.

8. Save and close the project.

NOTES

Conditional Actions

I hope you agree that up to this point, Actions have been sweet... as sweet as a caramel apple. But let's crank things up a notch or two with a slightly more complex Advanced Action. The previous project contains Standard Actions, a list of behaviors. Advanced Actions are more powerful than simply allowing multiple behaviors on a single object interaction. They can also perform different actions based on specific situations. These are called Conditional Actions.

Guided Activity 50: Create a Variable

1. Open the **ConditionalActionMe** project from the Captivate2019BeyondData folder.

2. Go to slide **3**.

   There is a **numberOfServings** variable just under the title, and there are other variables that display how much of each ingredient is needed. Captivate calculates these values in a conditional action based on the number of servings the learner requests.

3. Drag the Text Caption and the Smart Shape from the Scrap Area to the slide and position the objects until your slide is similar to the picture below.

   The Text Caption already has a name (**ZeroWarning**) and is not Visible in output. (You can confirm both by selecting the caption and observing the Properties Inspector.) Select the Smart Shape (the thought bubble) and notice that it is named **Tip** and is set to not be Visible in output. To manipulate the number of servings and the amount of each ingredient needed, you need to create a variable to store the learner input.

4. Create a Variable.

   ☐ choose **Project > Variables**

   The Variables dialog box opens.

   ☐ from the **Type** drop-down menu, ensure **User** is selected

   ☐ click the **Add New** button and then type **servingsRequested** into the **Name** field

❏ in the **Value** field, type **1**

❏ in the **Description** field, type **The number of servings desired input by the learner. Should be greater than 0. Used in the advanced action updateRecipe.**

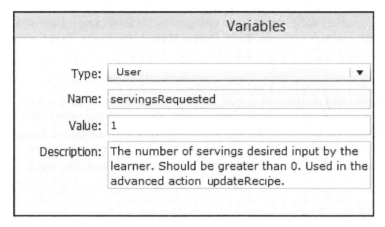

❏ click the **Save** button

❏ click the **Close** button

The new variable needs to be associated with the Text Entry Box so that when the learner types a number, the number is stored in the servingsRequested variable. Once stored, the number can be displayed later in the lesson or used by an Advanced Action to perform calculations.

5. Associate the new variable with an object on the slide.

❏ still working on slide **3**, select the **Text Entry Box** (it's at the bottom of the slide)

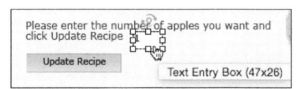

❏ on the **Properties Inspector**, select the **Style** tab

❏ from the **Variable** drop-down menu, select **servingsRequested** (this is the variable you just created)

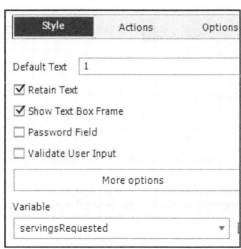

6. Review the purpose for some of the other variables.

☐ choose **Project > Variables**

You created one of the variables in the list (servingsRequested). Captivate comes with two user variables (cpQuizInfoStudentID and cpQuizInfoStudentName). Captivate automatically created another variable (**Text_Entry_Box_1**) when the Text Entry Box was inserted on the slide. I created the rest of the variables for you.

Before proceeding, let's ensure that you understand the role of each of the variables in the Caramel Apple recipe. As I mentioned above, the first variable, **Text_Entry_Box_1**, was created by Captivate automatically when I inserted the Text Entry Box onto slide 3. The rest of the variables can be broken down into two categories: the number of items needed for a single caramel apple and the number of items necessary to meet the **servingsRequested** by the learner. To determine how much of an ingredient is necessary, Captivate needs both of these pieces of information.

Text_Entry_Box_1
appleUnit
caramelUnit
cpQuizInfoStudentID
cpQuizInfoStudentName
milkUnit
numberOfApples
numberOfCaramels
numberOfServings
numberOfSticks
servingsRequested
stickUnit
teaspoonsOfMilk

Here is what the variables in the list do:

Single Serving Variables:

appleUnit: The number of apples for a single serving.

caramelUnit: The number of caramels for a single serving.

milkUnit: The number of teaspoons of milk for a single serving.

stickUnit: The number of sticks for a single serving.

Calculated Variables:

numberOfApples: The number of apples required for the desired servings of caramel apples.

numberOfCaramels: The number of caramels required for the desired servings of caramel apples.

teaspoonsOfMilk: The number of teaspoons of milk for the desired servings of caramel apples.

numberOfSticks: The number of sticks required for the desired servings of caramel apples.

numberOfServings: The number of servings of CaramelApples.

7. Close the Variables dialog box.

8. Keep the project open.

Guided Activity 51: Create a Conditional Action

1. Ensure that the **ConditionalActionMe** project is still open.

   It is time to begin creating the Advanced Action that calculates the amount of each ingredient needed and that displays the proper messages for either zero servings or a large number of servings. The new Advanced Action will be Conditional.

2. Create a Conditional Action.

   ☐ choose **Project > Advanced Actions**

   ☐ select the **Conditional Tab** check box

A conditional action contains three basic parts: a conditional check (IF area), a success case (Actions area within the IF area), and a failure case (Actions area within the ELSE area).

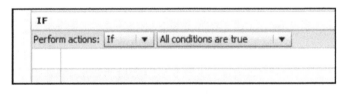

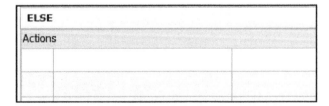

Here's how it works. If you were trying to decide what to do for lunch, you might go through a thought process like this:

```
IF

     is-it-lunchtime?(conditional check)
THEN

     drive to the nearest pizzeria(success case)
     order a giant pizza pie
     eat
ELSE

     keep working at my desk(failure case)
END
```

The condition is first evaluated. If the condition evaluates as TRUE, the behaviors in the success case are executed. Otherwise, the behaviors in the failure case are executed. The conditional check area may contain more than one item to check. For example, you may wish to check *is-it-lunchtime?* as well as *am-I-hungry?* You can evaluate both items and make a decision upon whatever combination of items you like.

Perhaps you require that it be lunchtime AND that you are hungry to go out for pizza. Or maybe because you are hungry regardless of the time of day OR if it is lunchtime regardless if you are hungry, you should go out for pizza. To set this option within Captivate, you need to select the correct option from the **Perform action if** drop-down menu (just below the IF bar).

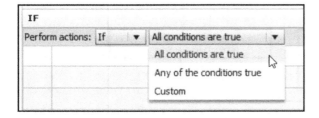

For this activity, I'll keep it as simple as possible and just check one condition.

NOTES

Before you start programming a conditional action, you should take a step back to analyze the goal of the action. The conditional action that you are about to create has three sections: (1) check if the servings requested is greater than 7, (2) check if the number of servings requested is a positive number and calculate ingredients and (3) show a glowing yield message. Often it is useful to sketch out a flowchart or jot down how you want the action to behave. A flowchart for this conditional action is shown below.

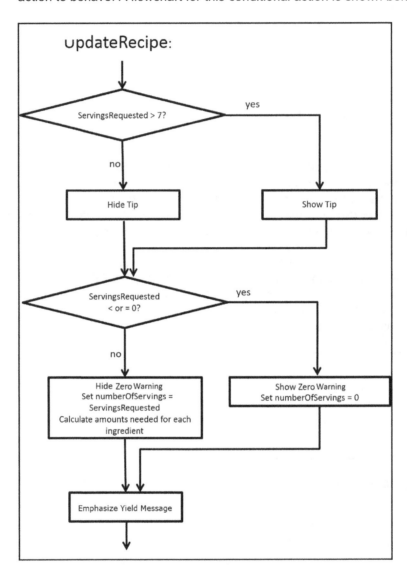

The first step is to create a conditional action that checks to see if the learner has input a serving size of at least 7. If so, the Action displays a tip message about how many caramels to melt at one time.

3. Create a conditional action.

   ☐ in the **Action Name** field, type **updateRecipe**

4. Confirm the Perform action.

   ☐ from the **Perform actions** drop-down menu, ensure **If** is selected from the first drop-down menu (the other option is **While**)

   ☐ ensure that **All conditions are true** is selected from the next drop-down menu

IF			
Perform actions:	If ▼	All conditions are true ▼	

5. Create a conditional check.

   ☐ double-click in the first row of the **IF** area

   ☐ from the first drop-down menu, choose **variable** (the variable drop-down menu changes to a list of variables)

   ☐ select **servingsRequested** from the list of variables

   ☐ from the **Select comparison operator** drop-down menu, choose **is greater than**

   ☐ from the next drop-down, choose **literal**

   ☐ type **7** and then press **[enter]** on your keyboard

IF			
Perform actions:	If ▼	All conditions are true ▼	
✓	servingsRequested	is greater than	7

   A literal value is an exact value, such as the number **7**; an exact name, such as **Biff**; or even an exact phrase, such as "**Actions are fun!**" A variable is something that does not have a set value and can change, like the number of servings requested (making it variable).

6. Create a success case.

   ☐ double-click the first row in the **Actions** area

   ☐ from the **Select Action** drop-down menu, choose **Show**

   ☐ from the drop-down menu, choose **Tip**

Actions		
✓	Show	Tip

   The update recipe button may be clicked several times. If the number of servings is not excessive, any tip remaining from the previous recipe update should be cleared (hidden). This is done in the ELSE area.

7. Create a failure case.

   ☐ at the bottom of the Advanced Actions dialog box, click the word **ELSE** to expand the ELSE area

   ☐ double-click the first row in the **ELSE Actions** area

   ☐ from the **Select Action** drop-down menu, choose **Hide**

   ☐ from the drop-down menu, choose **Tip**

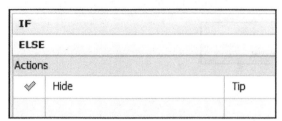

   ☐ click the **Save As Action** button

   ☐ click the **OK** button

   ☐ click the **Close** button

Conditional Actions Confidence Check

1. Still working in the **ConditionalActionMe** project, slide **3**, attach the **updateRecipe** Advanced Action to the **Update Recipe** button.

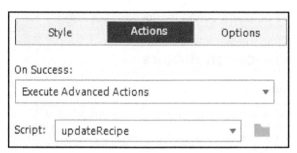

2. Preview the project.

3. Click the **Directions** button to move to slide **3**.

4. Type **22** into the Text Entry Box and then click the **Update Recipe** button.

   The **Tip** object should appear next to the little girl.

5. Type **3** into the Text Entry Box, and then click the **Update Recipe** button.

   The **Tip** object should disappear.

6. Close the preview.

Multiple Decision Blocks

A conditional action can contain numerous scenarios. These are known as Decision Blocks. Each Decision Block contains a separate set of IF/ELSE areas. In the flow chart on page 150, decisions are represented by diamonds. If you're going to have multiple scenarios (Decision Blocks), it's a good idea to name the blocks, which you'll be doing during the following activity.

Guided Activity 52: Create Decision Blocks

1. Ensure that the **ConditionalActionMe** project is still open.

2. Name the Decision Blocks.

   ☐ choose **Project > Advanced Actions**

   ☐ from the **Existing Actions** drop-down menu, choose **updateRecipe**

   ☐ double-click the word **Untitled-1** in the Decision Block area (it's the three rectangles above the Conditional tab check box)

   ☐ change the name to **ExcessCheck** and then press [**enter**] on your keyboard

   ☐ double-click the word **Untitled-2** on the middle Decision Block

   ☐ change the name to **Calculate** and then press [**enter**] on your keyboard

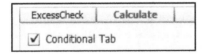

3. Set up a Decision Block.

   ☐ select the Calculate Decision Block

   The word **Calculate** should be blue indicating that you are editing that specific Decision Block.

   ☐ click the check box next to **Conditional Tab**

   ☐ double-click in the first row of the **IF** area

   ☐ choose **variable** from the first drop-down menu and then choose **servingsRequested**

   ☐ from the **Select comparison operator** drop-down menu, choose **lesser or equal to**

   ☐ from the **Variable** drop-down menu, choose **literal**

   ☐ type **0** and then press [**enter**]

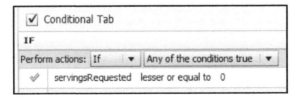

❑ in the **Actions** area, double-click in the first row

❑ from the **Select Action** drop-down menu, choose **Show**

❑ from the drop-down menu, choose **ZeroWarning**

Let's also set the numberOfServings variable now so that it displays correctly in the Yield Message.

❑ in the **Actions** area, double-click in the next blank row

❑ from the **Select Action** drop-down menu, choose **Assign**

❑ from the **Select Variable** drop-down menu, choose **numberOfServings**

❑ from the **Variable** drop-down menu, choose **literal**

❑ type a **0** and then press [**enter**]

Actions		
✅	Show	ZeroWarning
✅	Assign	numberOfServings with 0

If the number of servings requested is more than 0, it is time to create all of the calculations that are displayed in the recipe text caption. For each ingredient, you will multiply the number of that ingredient necessary for a single serving (*ingredient*Unit) by the number of servings desired (servingsRequested) and save that into the total amount for that ingredient (numberOf*Ingredient*).

4. Create a failure case.

❑ from the bottom of the Advanced Actions dialog box, click the word **ELSE** to expand the ELSE section

❑ double-click the **Actions** area

❑ from the **Select Action** drop-down menu, choose **Hide**

❑ from the drop-down menu, choose **ZeroWarning**

❑ double-click the next row

❑ from the **Select Action** drop-down menu, choose **Assign**

❑ from the **Select Variable** drop-down menu, choose **numberOfServings**

❑ from the **Variable** drop-down menu, choose **variable**

❑ from the drop-down menu, choose **servingsRequested**

❑ double-click the next row

❑ from the **Select Action** drop-down menu, choose **Expression**

❑ from the drop-down menu, choose **numberOfApples**

❑ from the **Variable** drop-down menu, choose **variable**

❑ from the drop-down menu, choose **appleUnit**

❑ from the **+** drop-down menu, choose *

❑ from the **Variable** drop-down menu, choose **variable**

NOTES

☐ from the drop-down menu, choose **servingsRequested**

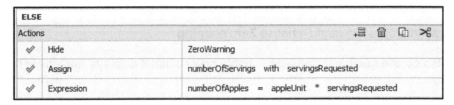

ELSE						
Actions			⊞	🗑	⎙	✂
✅	Hide	ZeroWarning				
✅	Assign	numberOfServings with servingsRequested				
✅	Expression	numberOfApples = appleUnit * servingsRequested				

5. Click the **Update Action** button.

6. Click the **OK** button.

7. Click the **Close** button to close the Action.

8. Save and close the project.

Decision Blocks Confidence Check

1. Open the **ConditionalActionMe_Part2** project from the Captivate2019BeyondData folder.

   You are just about done. The last thing left to do is add the little flicker effect to the Yield text. There are two choices here. The effect could be added to both the IF and the ELSE clauses of the Calculate decision block, but that seems inefficient because that would require you to add the same action in two places. It makes more sense to do it just once in its own decision block, one that is executed after the Calculate decision block.

2. Open the **Advanced Actions** dialog box.

3. Display the **UpdateRecipe** action.

4. On the Decision block list, **double-click** the third block and change the name to **Effect**.

5. Ensure that the Conditional Tab is NOT checked.

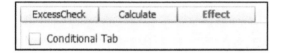

6. Double-click in the first row of the actions area.

7. From the **Select Action** drop-down menu, choose **Apply Effect**.

8. From the drop-down menu, choose **YieldMessage**.

9. From the **Select Effect** drop-down menu, choose **Emphasis > Flicker**.

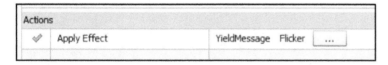

10. Click **Update Action** to save the action.

    Before you leave the Advance Action, look at the preview of your script by clicking the **Preview Action** button in the upper right of the dialog box.

This option is available only for conditional actions. It doesn't make any sense for standard actions because you can see an entire standard action on one screen and use your scroll bar if you have a large number of action statements. However, for a conditional action, which may contain numerous decision blocks, this feature is pretty cool (at least to the geek in all of us).

It is a good idea at this point to compare this code structure to the flow chart on page 150. After reviewing, if you find you need to move decision blocks around or insert or remove some, you can use the tools above the decision block list to shuffle things.

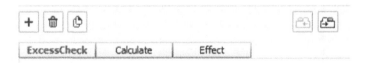

11. Close the Preview Actions dialog box.

12. Close the Advanced Actions dialog box.

13. Save your work and preview the project.

14. When finished previewing the project, close the preview.

Are you wondering why there is a slide **1** in the project that seems to have little value? And are you wondering how the images were hidden when the rewind button on the playbar was clicked? These two items go hand in hand. I created an Advanced Action called **reset**. Now that you are more comfortable with Advanced Actions, the role of the reset action (shown below) should make sense.

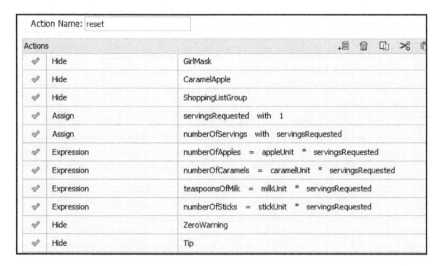

The **reset** action is executed upon entry to slide **2**. This is done on the Properties Inspector using the On Enter behavior in the Actions tab.

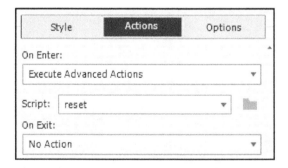

Now, about that first slide....

15. On the Timeline for slide **1**, notice that the slide is set to play for only a fraction of a second.

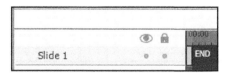

When you try to use an On Enter behavior on the first slide of a project, you don't always get the desired behavior. Creating a placeholder slide is a simple workaround. Making the second slide in a project behave as if it were the first slide ensures that the On Enter behavior is executed properly. Slide 1 in this case is simply a placeholder slide that has the same background as the second slide. The first slide plays for just a split second, which is not noticeable to the learner. When using this technique, be sure to remove any slide transitions so it appears as if two slides are just a single slide.

16. Save and close the project.

Notes

Module 8: Masters, Themes, and Templates

In This Module You Will Learn About:

And You Will Learn To:

Master Slides

If you need to add recurring features to your slides (such as your logo, background colors, copyright notices, etc.), setting up and using Captivate's master slides feature is the ideal strategy. Instead of manually copying and pasting recurring objects onto slides, you can add them to a master slide one time. After that, it's a simple matter of applying a master slide to selected Filmstrip slides and the Filmstrip slides will instantly look like the Master Slide. Best of all, if you modify the Master Slide, any Filmstrip slides using the edited Master Slide instantly get updated automatically.

Each new Adobe Captivate project contains one Main Master Slide and multiple Content Master Slides. You can format the Main Master Slide, format the existing Content Master Slides, or create your own Content Master Slides.

Guided Activity 53: Work With the Main Master Slide

1. Open **MasterMe** from the Captivate2019BeyondData folder.

2. Copy an image from slide 1 for use on a Master Slide.

   ❏ on the Filmstrip, select slide **1**

   ❏ right-click the "S" logo on the slide and choose **Copy**

3. Open the Master Slide Panel.

   ❏ choose **Window > Master Slide**

   The Filmstrip is replaced with the Master Slide panel. The first slide, and the largest, is the Main Master Slide. There is only one Main Master Slide per Captivate project. The remaining master slides are Content Master Slides.

4. Paste the logo onto the Main Master Slide.

   ❏ on the **Master Slide panel**, select the **Main Master Slide**

   ❏ choose **Edit > Paste**

The logo shows up on the Main Master Slide and on *every* Content Master Slide.

5. Exit the Master.

☐ on the toolbar at the top of the Captivate window, click **Exit Master**

The logo appears on *every* Filmstrip slide. If you want an object to appear in the same location on every slide throughout the project, adding it to the Main Master Slide works great. Because the Main Master Slide affects every slide in the project, its most common use is for background colors and/or images.

In this instance, pasting the logo on the Main Master Slide is overkill because the logo is already appearing on the first and last slides in the project. You'll need to find a way to add the logo via Master Slides without affecting every slide in the project.

6. Return to the Master Slide panel (**Window > Master Slide** or, on the Properties Inspector, click the **Master slide view** button).

7. Delete the logo from the Main Master Slide

8. Exit the Master Slides view.

The logo has been removed from every Filmstrip slide except the first and last slides. (These slides had the logo before you opened the project.)

As you've seen, the Main Master Slide is powerful. Changes made to the Main Master get applied to all Filmstrip slides. If you want to alter the appearance of specific Filmstrip slides efficiently, you'll need to leverage the Content Masters. You'll do that next.

Note: The SSS logo should still be copied to your clipboard. If you copied another item to the clipboard in the interim, go back to slide 1 now and re-copy the logo to the clipboard. (You'll be pasting the logo onto a Content Master Slide during the next activity.)

Guided Activity 54: Work With Content Masters

1. Ensure that the **MasterMe** project is still open.

2. Return to the Master Slide panel (**Window > Master Slide**).

3. Insert a Content Master Slide.

   ☐ choose **Insert > Content Master Slide**

   A new Content Master Slide is added after the existing Content Master named Blank.

4. Name the new Content Master Slide.

   ☐ with the new Content Master Slide selected, use the Properties Inspector to name the Content Master Slide **LogoLowerRight**

   On the Master Slide panel, the new Content Master Slide should now display the LogoLowerRight name.

5. Add the logo to the new Content Master Slide.

   ❑ right-click the **LogoLowerRight** Content Master Slide and choose **Edit > Paste**

   The logo that you copied earlier should appear on the LogoLowerRight Content Master. If not, Exit the Master, copy the logo on Filmstrip slide 1, return to the LogoLowerRight Content Master, and paste again.

6. Drag the logo to the lower right of the LogoLowerRight Content Master Slide.

7. Exit the Master Slide view.

   Because you have not yet applied the LogoLowerRight master to any of the Filmstrip slides, none of the Filmstrip slides are displaying the logo in the lower right.

8. Save your work.

Guided Activity 55: Apply a Master to Filmstrip Slides

1. Ensure that the **MasterMe** project is still open.

2. Apply a Content Master Slide to Filmstrip slides.

   ☐ on the Filmstrip, select slide **2**

   Notice that slide **2** does not yet have the logo you added to the LogoLowerRight Content Master Slide. That will change the instant you apply the LogoLowerRight Content Master Slide to this (or any) Filmstrip slide.

   ☐ ensure that slide 2 is still selected

   ☐ press the [**shift**] key on your keyboard

   ☐ select slide **9**

   ☐ release the [**shift**] key

   Slides **2** through **9** should now be selected.

   ☐ on the Properties Inspector, select **LogoLowerRight** from the Master Slide drop-down menu

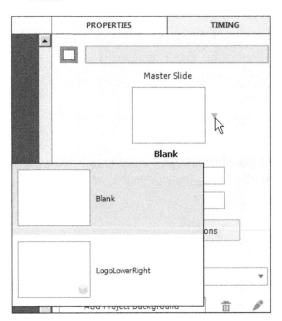

   The **LogoLowerRight** Content Master Slide is applied to the selected Filmstrip slides. When you go from slide to slide, you'll see the logo in the lower right corner of every slide (except the first and last slide).

3. Save your work.

Guided Activity 56: Edit a Content Master Slide

1. Ensure that the **MasterMe** project is still open.

2. Return to the Master Slide panel.

3. Reposition the logo on the **LogoLowerRight** Master Slide.

   ☐ on the Master Slide panel, select the **LogoLowerRight** Content Master

   ☐ select the **logo**

   ☐ on the **Properties Inspector**, select the **Options** tab

   ☐ from the **Transform** area, change the **X** value to **523**

   ☐ change the **Y** value to **366**

4. Exit the Master Slide view.

   The change you made to the **LogoLowerRight** Content Master Slide has instantly been applied to the Filmstrip slides that are using the LogoLowerRight Master Slide.

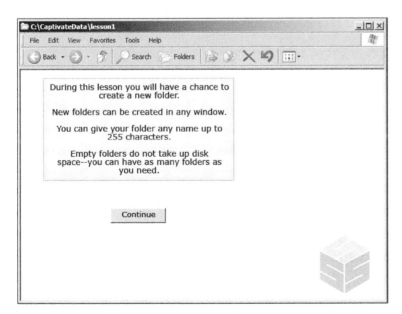

Masters Confidence Check

1. Return to the Master slide view.

2. Select the LogoLowerRight Content Master Slide and choose **Edit > Duplicate**.

   There should be two Content Master Slides named LogoLowerRight.

3. Rename the newest LogoLowerRight Content Master Slide as **Logo and Copyright**.

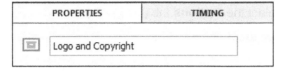

4. With the **Logo and Copyright** Content Master Slide selected, insert a text caption.

5. Delete the placeholder text from the new caption.

6. On the Properties Inspector, click the **Insert Symbol** tool.

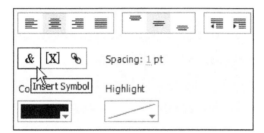

7. Select **Copyright** from the list of symbols.

8. Type **2019, All Rights Reserved.** after the copyright symbol.

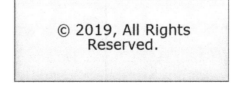

9. Using the Properties Inspector, change the Caption Type to **transparent** and change the Font to **Verdana, 10 pt**.

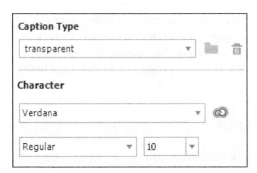

10. Change the alignment of the copyright text to **Align Right**.

11. Position the logo and the copyright notice in the lower right of the master slide (similar to the image below).

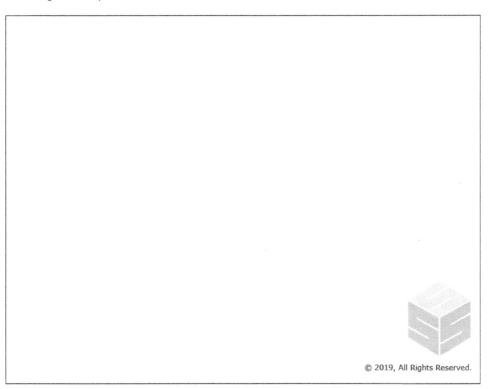

© 2019, All Rights Reserved.

12. Exit the Master slide view.

13. Apply the **Logo and Copyright** Master Slide to project Slides 2 through 9. (You learned how to do this on page 164.)

14. Save your work and close the project.

NOTES

Themes

Earlier in this module, you learned how master slides can help ensure consistent placement of repetitive slide objects throughout a project. A Theme is a collection of slide elements, master slides, object styles, and project skins designed to give your project a consistent look and feel. Captivate ships with several Themes. You can edit and save the provided Themes, or you can create your own. You can choose to apply a theme to a new project or to apply a Theme to any existing project at any time.

Guided Activity 57: Apply a Theme

1. Open **ThemeMe** from the Captivate2019BeyondData folder.

2. Go from slide to slide and notice that this project has ample content, but the overall look and feel of the project leaves plenty to be desired.

3. Apply a Theme to the project.

   ☐ click the **Themes** icon on the toolbar (not the Themes menu) and choose **Coastal**

   Note: You won't see Theme names until you hover over them.

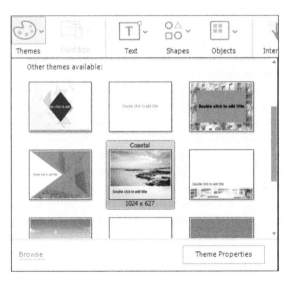

Because the Object Styles used in each Theme look different, you are asked to confirm the action.

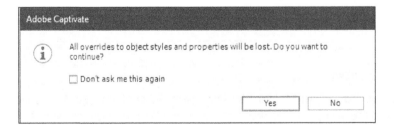

   ☐ click the **Yes** button

After a few seconds, a bit of magic takes place and every slide in the project is formatted to match the Theme.

Applying Themes Confidence Check

1. Spend a few moments applying some of the other available Themes to the project.

2. Apply the **Dynamic** theme to the project.

Adobe Captivate: Creating Software Simulations

3. Using the Filmstrip, scroll through the slides and notice that most of the slides have formatting issues (this project doesn't need the subtitle and the text placeholders aren't set up to allow for optimum formatting). You'll take care of those issues next as you learn to customize a theme.

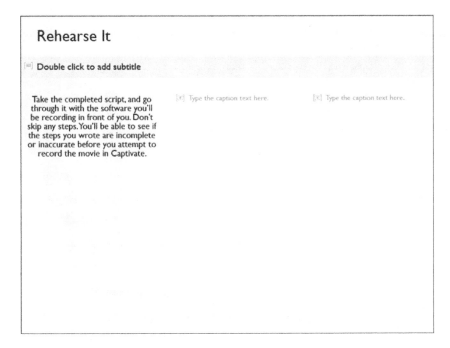

Rehearse It

Double click to add subtitle

Take the completed script, and go through it with the software you'll be recording in front of you. Don't skip any steps. You'll be able to see if the steps you wrote are incomplete or inaccurate before you attempt to record the movie in Captivate.

Type the caption text here.   Type the caption text here.

4. Save your work. (Keep the project open for the next activity.)

Guided Activity 58: Create a Custom Theme

1. Ensure that the **ThemeMe** project is open and that you're using the **Dynamic** theme.

2. On slide **1**, notice that the heading is a bit low on the slide.

3. On slide **3**, notice there is a subheading you don't need and the body text positioning on the slide needs work.

4. Edit a Content Master Slide.

   ☐ go to **Master Slide** view (Window > Master Slide)

   ☐ select the **Title** Content Master (the first slide on the Filmstrip is using this Content Master)

   ☐ resize and reposition the title placeholder so that it is positioned on the slide similar to what is shown below

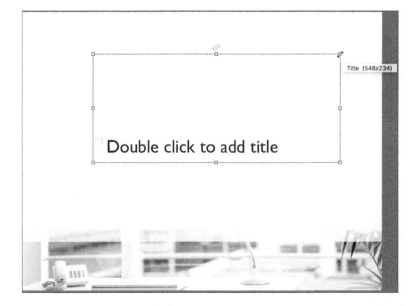

5. Edit another Content Master Slide.

☐ select the **Content 03** Content Master (the remaining Filmstrip slides are using this Content Master slide)

☐ **delete** the **subtitle** placeholder from the slide

☐ drag the **Title** placeholder down two to three inches

☐ resize and reposition the remaining caption placeholders similar to the image below

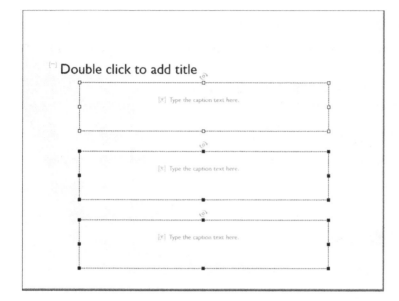

6. Exit the Master View.

7. Reset a Master Slide.

☐ on the **Filmstrip**, select slide **1**

It's possible that the title you repositioned on the master slide has not yet moved on the Filmstrip slide. In that case, you can force the issue by resetting the Master Slide.

☐ on the **Properties Inspector**, click **Reset Master Slide**

The **Title** Slide master is reapplied to slide 1, and the slide format is adjusted to match the edits made to the content master.

8. Reset a Master Slide on another Filmstrip slide.

   ❑ on the Filmstrip, select slides **2** through **10** (pressing [**shift**] on your keyboard and clicking the first and last slides in the range works best)

   ❑ on the **Properties Inspector**, click **Reset Master Slide**

   The formatting for all of the selected slides changes to reflect the edits you made to the content master.

9. Save the changes to the Theme as a new Theme.

   ❑ from the **Themes** menu (not the Themes icon on the toolbar), choose **Save Theme As**

   ❑ name the theme **YourFirstNameTheme** and **save** it to the **Captivate2019BeyondData** folder

   ❑ click the **OK** button to acknowledge the successfully saved Theme

10. Observe your Theme in the Themes panel.

    ❑ from the toolbar, click **Themes**

    Your Theme appears on the Themes panel along with the original Themes. It can now be used by any new project or any existing project.

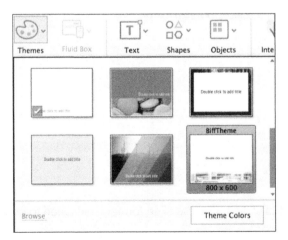

11. Apply a different theme to the project.

12. Reapply your custom theme to the ThemeMe project.

Custom Themes Confidence Check

1. Return to the Master slide view and select the **Title** content master.

2. Select the title placeholder and on the Properties Inspector, change the Character to **Arial** and the size to **36**.

3. With the Title placeholder still selected, click the menu to the right of Style Name and choose **Save changes to Existing Style**.

4. Select the **Content 03** Content Master.

5. Change the font for the Title to **Arial** and then save the changes to the style.

6. Change the font for the Caption style to **Arial** and then save the changes to the style.

7. Make any other formatting changes you like to either the appearance of the master slides or the styles.

8. When finished, return to the Filmstrip.

9. Save and close the project.

10. Create a New, Blank project.

    By default, new projects use the Pearl theme.

11. Use the Themes icon to apply your custom theme to the project.

12. Close the new project (there is no need to save it).

Templates

To ensure that new Captivate projects are consistently formatted (not only your projects, but projects created by other developers on your team), it's a good idea to use Themes (see page 170). As you have already seen earlier in this module, Themes include master slides, object styles, and master slide object placeholders. But Themes are limited. You cannot control the size of a project with a Theme, nor can you use a Theme to control the size of a new software simulation. Because of the shortcomings inherent with Themes, Templates offer an ideal upgrade.

Templates, which use a **cptl** extension instead of the standard **cptx** extension, can contain multiple master slides and object styles, just like Themes. However, unlike Themes, templates can contain placeholder slides, Filmstrip slides with reusable content, placeholder quiz slides, variables, widgets, advanced actions, custom skins, Project Information, start and end properties, and more.

Once you've created a template, you can use the template when you create each new project. If you use the template workflow, each new project will look exactly like the template, ensuring consistency among all new projects.

Guided Activity 59: Review a Template

1. Open **Finished_S3_ProjectTemplate** from the Captivate2019BeyondData folder.

   Notice that the project's name includes a **cptl** extension (this extension is used only by Captivate templates).

2. Ensure you are on slide **1**.

   The slide contains a few graphics, a Begin button, and a Title placeholder. When used as the starting point for a new project, the title placeholder gets replaced with actual content. The title's slide position, font, and font size have already been determined by the person who created the template.

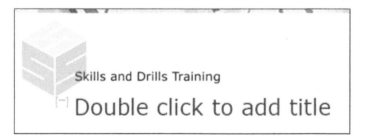

3. Go to slide **2**.

   Slide 2 is a Recording Slide Placeholder. You'll soon be able to double-click the placeholder and immediately begin recording screen actions.

4. Review some of the Object Styles used in the template.

   ☐ choose **Edit > Object Style Manager**

   The template includes several custom Object Styles. SSS Default Text Caption is also set to be the default caption used whenever a caption is inserted onto a slide.

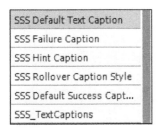
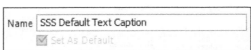

   ☐ click the **Cancel** button

5. Switch to Master slide view.

   The template includes two custom Content Master Slides: **LogoLowerRight** and **Logo and Copyright**. You learned how to create these kinds of master slides on page 164.

6. Return to Filmstrip view.

7. Review the Skin.

   ☐ choose **Project > Skin Editor**

   The template is using a custom skin complete with a playbar with colors edited to match the colors on the slide's background.

8. Close the Skin Editor.

---

9. Review the Project Information.

❐ choose **File > Project Info**

The information about Super Simplistic Solutions has already been filled in. When the template is used as a project, all that the developer needs to do is update the fields.

10. Review the Start and End properties.

❐ from the left of the Preferences dialog box, **Project** group, select **Start and End**

Notice that a Preloader has already been specified. In addition, the Preloader % is already set to 50%. At the bottom of the dialog box, notice the **Fade** and **Project End options** have also been set.

❐ click the **Cancel** button

This template looks pretty much ready to go. All you need to do is create a new project that uses the template, and you'll be off to the races.

11. Close the template (do not save any changes if prompted).

Guided Activity 60: Create a Project Based on a Template

1. Create a new project based on an existing template.

   ❏ choose **File > New Project > Project From Template**

   The Open dialog appears. You'll need to help Captivate find the template you were just exploring.

   ❏ navigate to the **Captivate2019BeyondData** folder and open the **Finished_S3_ProjectTemplate**

   A moment ago you spent some time looking at different aspects of the template. The extension used by the template is **cptl**. Check out the name of this project: it's an untitled project with a **cptx** extension. When you open the template via Project From Template, the resulting file is a standard Captivate project that is an exact replica of the template. Unlike some programs that use templates, there is not a link (or relationship) between the template and the project. If you were to reopen and edit the template now, the changes would not be reflected in this or any project based on the template. Conversely, any change made to a project has no effect on the template used to create it.

2. Replace the Title Placeholder with text.

   ❏ on slide 1, double-click the title placeholder

   ❏ **Templates are Awesome!**

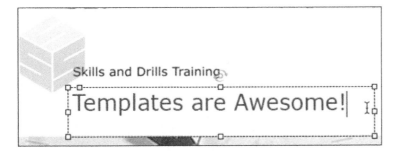

3. Record a series of screen actions using the Recording Slide Placeholder.

   ❏ go to slide **2**

   ❏ double-click the words **Double-click to start recording**

   The untitled project disappears, and you are taken into Captivate's recording mode.

   ❏ select any program you like from the drop-down menu (if nothing is available, create a recording of your desktop or start any application to capture)

   ❏ ensure that **Snap to Window** is selected

   ❏ from the **Recording Type** area, ensure **Automatic** is selected

☐ from the **Mode** drop-down menu, ensure **Demo** is selected

☐ **Panning** should be set to **No Panning** and **Audio** set to **No Narration**

☐ click the **Record** button

4. After the 3-2-1 countdown, click a few things in the application you elected to record. (It really doesn't matter what you click because you won't be keeping the recording for more than a few seconds.)

5. When finished, stop the recording process.

   The recorded slides have been added to your new project. The text captions that were created during the recording process are already using the SSS Default Text Caption set up in the template. Nice! You could now move on and record more lessons using the template or spend time producing and publishing this lesson. Because this was just a demo showing how to use a Captivate template, you won't be saving this project.

6. Preview the project.

7. When finished, close the preview and close the project without saving.

Guided Activity 61: Create a Project Template

1. Create a new project template.

   ☐ **File > New Project > Project Template**

   The New Project Template dialog box opens. This is where you set up the width and height of the template. Once you select a width and height, all of the projects and screen recordings you create with the template will use this size.

   ☐ from the **Select** drop-down menu, choose **1280 x 720**

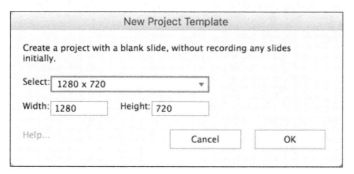

   ☐ click the **OK** button

   An untitled template opens. Notice that the file contains a **cptl** extension just like the template you opened and used earlier.

2. Save the project template to the Captivate2019BeyondData folder as **MyCaptivateTemplate**.

3. Apply a Theme to the template.

   ☐ on the toolbar, click **Themes** and choose **Coastal**

4. Add a Lesson Overview slide.

   ☐ choose **Insert > New Slide from > Content 07**

   ☐ replace the subtitle placeholder with **Lesson Overview**

5. Duplicate a slide.

   ☐ right-click slide 2 and choose **Duplicate**

   ☐ on slide **3**, replace the word **Overview** with **Review**

6. Insert a Recording Slide Placeholder

☐ select slide **2**

☐ choose **Insert > Placeholder slides > Recording Slide Placeholder**

7. Insert a Question Slide Placeholder

☐ select slide **3**

☐ choose **Insert > Placeholder slides > Question Slide Placeholder**

Your template now has five slides complete with placeholder objects and placeholder slides.

Template Confidence Check

1. Display the Preferences dialog box.

2. From the **Project > Start and End** category, select a **Preloader** from Captivate's Gallery or, if you have access to an image of your own, you can use it as the Preloader.

3. Set the **Preloader %** to **50**.

4. Save and close the template.

5. Create a new project **based on your new template**.

6. Save the new project as **MyProjectBasedOnMyTemplate**.

7. Use the Recording Slide Placeholder to record a quick software simulation (it can be a recording of any computer process you like).

8. Use the Question Slide Placeholder to insert a few question slides into the project (a few multiple choice and True/False questions).

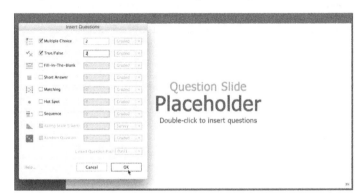

9. If you'd like, add a few made-up questions and answers on the questions slides. (Keep in mind that if you want to add answers to the question slides, you'll need to work on the Quiz inspector.)

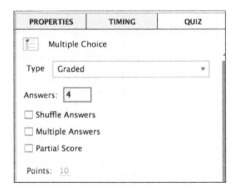

10. Save and close the project.

    Note: The template you created was based on the Coastal Theme. If you don't like the look of something in the template (the appearance of question slides for instance), you would close the project without saving (you haven't done much work to the project so you're not wasting any effort), open the **MyCaptivateTemplate.cptl** file, and make the appropriate edits to the Master Slides, Object Styles, or both.

Notes

iCONLOGiC
"Skills and Drills" Learning

Module 9: Responsive Projects

In This Module You Will Learn About:

- Responsive eLearning Development, page 186
- Breakpoint Mode, page 192
- Fluid Box Mode, page 204

And You Will Learn To:

- Review a Responsive Project, page 186
- Customize Breakpoints, page 188
- Save a Standard Project As Responsive, page 204
- Create a Responsive Project, page 192
- Use the Position Inspector, page 193
- Modify a Single Breakpoint, page 196
- Exclude from View, page 197
- Add a New Breakpoint, page 199
- Position and Smart Position Objects, page 200
- Edit Breakpoint Object Styles, page 203
- Insert and Name Fluid Boxes, page 207
- Resize Fluid Boxes, page 209
- Add Content to Fluid Boxes, page 210

Responsive eLearning Development

As an eLearning developer, you will likely need to create courses that can be accessed by all kinds of devices. The size of the screen that learners use to access eLearning lessons can vary widely. Consider the size of a typical smart phone compared to the various shapes and sizes of tablets, such as the Apple iPad, Microsoft Surface, and Amazon Kindle Fire. You could develop multiple Captivate projects that contain the same content but are sized to work on specific devices; however, you'd have to maintain, edit, and update those projects. Additionally, who could possibly consider every screen size for every device? Even if you could build lessons for every screen size known today, what about the screen sizes for devices that have yet to be invented?

As an alternative to managing multiple Captivate projects, you can create a single, responsive project that provides optimal viewing and an effective, unique, learning experience across a wide range of devices and screen sizes.

In a responsive project, the content seen by the learner doesn't just scale (get bigger or smaller as the size and orientation of the learner's display changes), the content can actually reflow or change altogether.

During this module, you will learn how to navigate Captivate's responsive interface (which is very different than working in a standard project). You will also learn how to create responsive projects from scratch.

You will learn how to use both of Captivate's responsive modes: **Breakpoints** and **Fluid Boxes**. Between the two modes, Fluid Boxes are easier to use but less flexible (you'll get a chance to use them on page 207); Breakpoint projects, which you'll work with first, allow for more accurate layouts but are more labor intensive to create.

Guided Activity 62: Review a Responsive Project

1. Open **ResponsiveScenarioMe** from the Captivate2019BeyondData folder.

   This project was created using Breakpoint mode.

2. Preview the project.

   When you preview a responsive project created using Breakpoint mode, you are taken into an HTLM5 browser window. There are three buttons (**Breakpoints**) at the top of the preview window. (A Breakpoint is the point at which the layout changes size to accommodate a different screen size.)

   When clicked, the buttons display the eLearning lesson at different screen sizes. The three Breakpoints in this project are 1024, 768, and 360. The person who developed this project set these Breakpoints based on the size of the screens their learners were anticipated to use. The Breakpoints represent a desktop or laptop user (1024), a Tablet user (768), and a Mobile user (360). When developing responsive projects, you can create up to five Breakpoints. It is up to you to set up the most common Breakpoints for your learners.

3. View the lesson at different screen sizes using the Breakpoints.

   ☐ with the preview window still open, click the **768** Breakpoint

   Rather than simply scaling the lesson so it fits on the smaller screen, the layout automatically *responds* to accommodate the available real estate (the background image is cropped, the text gets smaller and reflows).

   ☐ click the **360** Breakpoint

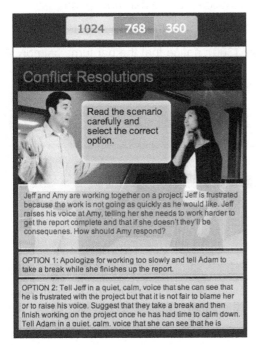

The preview at this Breakpoint is even more dramatic. A learner using a device this small would see something different than someone using a 1024 or 768 screen size, even though the content is the same.

4. Preview additional screen sizes.

   ☐ at the top of the preview window, below the Breakpoints, drag the slider left or right

As you drag the slider, the preview changes to show how the lesson will look on just about any screen size available today. In addition, the screen size is displayed in the middle of your slide.

5. Close the browser window.

6. Keep the project open for the next activity.

NOTES

Guided Activity 63: Customize Breakpoints

1. Ensure that the **ResponsiveScenarioMe** project is still open.

2. Change your magnification to **Best Fit** (View > Magnification).

3. Review the Breakpoints.

   ☐ select the **Desktop** Breakpoint (1024); notice that the bar turns purple

   ☐ select the **Tablet Portrait** Breakpoint (768); notice that the bar turns green

   ☐ select the **Mobile Portrait** Breakpoint (360); notice that the bar turns salmon

   You will learn the significance of the different color bars later.

   As you alternate among the different Breakpoints, the objects on the slide also change position. Note that only the objects within the colored horizontal bar will appear in the published lesson.

   Although the default Breakpoints are based on typical sizes of a desktop, tablet, and smart phone, you can easily adjust both the width and the height of any Breakpoint.

4. Manually adjust Breakpoints.

   ☐ if necessary, select the **Mobile Portrait** Breakpoint

   ☐ drag either Slider to decrease the width to **320** pixels (alternatively, you can highlight the number next to the left slider and type 320)

   Next you will adjust the Device Height. The ability to adjust a layout's height is disabled by default so that you don't accidentally change it. Each layout's default height provides space for Captivate's playbar. If you are not going to use a playbar in the published lesson, you should adjust the height accordingly.

5. Change the project Magnification to 75% (View > Magnification).

   If you are too close to the slide, you will not be able to see the new height you are about to set. I've found that 75% is almost always the perfect magnification, but you may need to test several magnification levels to find the perfect magnification for your display.

6. Adjust the Device Height.

☐ ensure you are on the **Mobile Portrait** Breakpoint and then, on the **Properties Inspector**, **Style** tab click **Device Height**

☐ from the bottom of the slide, drag the **Height Adjuster** (shown circled below) down to **460**

Note: When dragging the Height Adjuster, be careful not to grab slide objects by mistake. If you are having trouble dragging just the Height Adjuster, consider locking the image on the slide prior to dragging the Height Adjuster. (You can lock items via the far left of the Timeline.) Alternatively, you can type Height values directly into the field to the right of Device Height.

7. Look for changes on the other Breakpoints.

☐ select the **Tablet Portrait** Breakpoint

☐ select the **Desktop** Breakpoint

Even though you changed the height on the Mobile Portrait Breakpoint, the height on the other two Breakpoints did not change.

Next you will adjust the **Slide Height** independent of the **Device Height**. This technique is important if you need more real estate on your slide but do not want to change the Device Height.

Note: Changing the Slide Height adds a scroll bar to the published lesson if the viewing device is not the same aspect ratio as the slide.

8. Change Slide Height.

❑ select the **Mobile Portrait** Breakpoint

❑ on the **Properties Inspector**, **Style** tab, notice there is a link symbol to the right of **Device Height**

❑ click the link symbol to **Unlink from the Device height**

❑ change the **Slide Height** (careful, **not** the Device Height) to **660**

Notice that the Device Height at the top of the slide does not change; you've just added more real estate on your slide to add more objects. As mentioned earlier, when you publish the project, Captivate adds a scroll bar to the lesson so learners can scroll to see any content you added below the device height.

9. Link the Slide Height back to the Device Height.

❑ on the Properties Inspector, **Style** tab, click the link symbol to **Link to Device Height**

The Slide Height once again matches the Device Height (460 px).

Note: When you are determining your Breakpoint sizes, it is helpful to know the viewport sizes (device sizes) of devices by manufacturer. If you want to see a particular device size, visit **viewportsizes.mattstow.com**. If you want to see the size of the device you are using right now, visit **https://whatismyviewport.com/**.

Breakpoints Confidence Check

1. Ensure that the **ResponsiveScenarioMe** project is still open.

2. Adjust the **Desktop** Breakpoint Width to **1280**.

3. Adjust the **Desktop Device Height** to **720**.

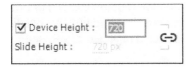

4. Adjust the **Tablet Portrait** Breakpoint width to **1024**.

5. Adjust the **Tablet Portrait** Device Height to **768**.

6. Close the project (there is no need to save it).

NOTES

Breakpoint Mode

The process of creating a responsive project from scratch is nearly identical to creating a standard project. However, in a standard project, each of the slides must be the same size so you are prompted to specify an overall project size when creating a new blank project. When you create a new responsive project you aren't asked to decide on a project size. Instead, you'll control the size of each Breakpoint (layout) on a case-by-case basis.

By default, new responsive projects use Fluid Boxes. As you'll see later in this module, Fluid Boxes are easy to use. However, with ease of use comes a loss of layout precision. If you need to control exactly where page elements appear based on a specific screen size, working with Breakpoints is your best bet.

Adding objects to a responsive project isn't any different than adding objects to a standard project. However, because responsive projects consist of multiple Breakpoints, the position of slide objects may need to be adjusted for each Breakpoint layout. You'll use the Position Inspector to control an object's slide position.

Guided Activity 64: Create a Responsive Project

1. Create a new Responsive Project.

   ☐ choose **File > New Project > Responsive Project**

   If this is your first time creating a responsive project in Captivate, a video of the process opens automatically. If the video and demo project opened, you can watch the video. When finished, close the video and then close the demo project. Then repeat the step above to create a **new responsive project**.

2. Save the project to the Captivate2019BeyondData folder as **MyBreakpointMode**.

3. Switch to Breakpoint Mode.

   ☐ choose **Project > Switch to Breakpoint Mode**

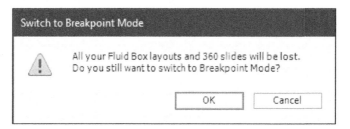

   ☐ click the **OK** button to agree to the switch and **save** the project again

   ☐ click the **Replace** button (Mac) or **Yes** button (PC) to replace the existing MyBreakpointMode project

Guided Activity 65: Use the Position Inspector

1. Ensure that the **MyBreakpointMode** project is still open.

2. Select the Desktop layout.

3. Insert a Character.

   ❑ choose **Media > Characters**

   ❑ double-click a **Character** group

   ❑ select a **pose**

   ❑ from the right side of the dialog box, select **Full**

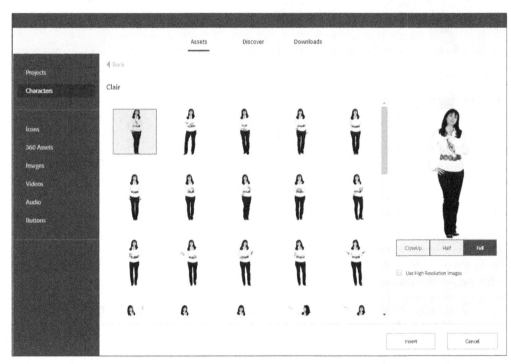

   ❑ click the **Insert** button

The character is inserted in the middle of the slide.

   ❑ drag the character to the bottom **left** of the slide

NOTES

4. Review the character's position on the other Breakpoints.

  ☐ select the **Tablet Portrait** Breakpoint

  ☐ select the **Mobile Portrait** Breakpoint

On the Mobile Portrait layout, the Character is not only smaller, but is also positioned at the top of the slide instead of the bottom. Initially, this automatic adjustment of objects seems fine. However, if you'd like an object (like the character) to remain fixed in a specific location, you need to adjust its Position Properties.

5. Select the **Desktop** Breakpoint

  ☐ change the view Magnification to Best Fit so you can see the entire slide. (**View > Magnification**)

6. Adjust the character's slide position.

  ☐ on the slide, double-click the character to open the **Properties Inspector**

A responsive project introduces a third inspector: the **Position Inspector**.

  ☐ on the **Position Inspector**, click the **Bottom** drop-down menu and choose **%**

  ☐ replace the existing **Bottom** value with **2** and press [**enter**]

  ☐ click the **Right** drop-down menu and choose **%**

  ☐ replace the existing value with **0** and press [**enter**]

The character moves 2% from the bottom of the slide and 0% from the right side of the slide.

7. Review each of the project's Breakpoints.

   Although the image now stays at the bottom right of each slide, the image still gets smaller as you move from Breakpoint to Breakpoint. Notice on the Position Inspector, Object Size area, that the default Object Size **Height** is set to Auto and **Width** is set to percent. To keep the Character the same size in all three layouts, you need to make another adjustment.

8. Adjust an object's Height and Width.

   ☐ select the **Desktop** Breakpoint

   ☐ select the character

   ☐ on the **Position Inspector**, **Object Size** area, change Width to **Auto**

   ☐ change the **Height** to **%**

   By setting an object's Height or Width to **Auto**, the object maintains its proportions from layout to layout.

9. Review each of the project's Breakpoints.

10. Adjust an object's position using pixels.

    ☐ select the **Desktop** layout

    ☐ select the character

    ☐ on the **Position Inspector**, **Object Size** area, keep the Width set to **Auto**

    ☐ change the Height to **px** (pixels)

11. Review each of the project's Breakpoints.

    By using **pixels** for the Height instead of a percentage, the image maintains its original size from layout to layout. However, notice on the Mobile Portrait layout that the image is now so big that it doesn't work with the layout. You'll adjust the position of the character on just the Mobile Portrait layout next.

Guided Activity 66: Modify a Single Breakpoint

1. Ensure that the **MyBreakpointMode** project is still open.

2. Adjust an object on a single layout.

   ☐ select the **Mobile Portrait** layout

   ☐ drag the character **down and to the right** so that only the top half of the image remains on the slide

3. Review each of the project's other views (Breakpoints).

   Notice that the change you made to the character on the Mobile Portrait slide has not affected the character on the other Breakpoints.

4. Select the **Mobile Portrait** view.

   With the character still selected, notice on the Position Inspector that the Object Position properties are **salmon**, while the Object Size properties are **purple**. The salmon color indicates properties that are unique to Mobile Portrait; purple indicates properties that are coming from the Desktop Breakpoint.

Guided Activity 67: Exclude from View

1. Ensure that the **MyBreakpointMode** project is still open.

2. Move an object to the Scrap Area.

   ☐ on the **Mobile Portrait** view, drag the character to the Scrap Area (the area outside the slide)

   The character will not preview or publish when it is positioned on the Scrap Area. Let's see what's happened to the character on the other views.

3. Review each of the project's views.

   Even though you positioned the character on the Scrap Area on the Mobile Portrait layout, the character still appears on both the Desktop and Tablet Portrait layouts.

   Breakpoints have a parent (Desktop) to child (Tablet Portrait) to grandchild (Mobile Portrait) relationship. When you edit an object on the Desktop layout, the change will be seen on all of the views. However, if you edit an object on the Tablet Portrait layout, the edit appears only on the Tablet Portrait and Mobile Portrait views (not the Desktop layout). When you edit an object on the Mobile Portrait layout, the edit appears only on the Mobile Portrait layout, not the other layouts.

   Manually dragging an object to the Scrap Area as a way of excluding it from a layout works great. But what if you want to exclude an object from multiple layouts at one time? Let's check out the Exclude from Other Views option.

4. Exclude an object from multiple views.

   ☐ select the **Tablet Portrait** Breakpoint

   ☐ choose **Shapes > Star**

☐ draw the star anywhere on the slide

☐ right click on the star and choose **Exclude from Other Views**

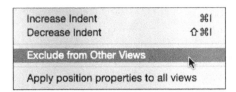

Increase Indent	⌘[
Decrease Indent	⇧⌘[
Exclude from Other Views	
Apply position properties to all views	

5. Review each of the project's Breakpoints.

   The star is automatically positioned on the Scrap Area for both the Desktop and Mobile Portrait views.

Guided Activity 68: Add a New Breakpoint

1. Ensure that the **MyBreakpointMode** project is still open.

2. Add a new Breakpoint.

   ☐ from between the Desktop and Tablet Portrait Breakpoints, click the **plus sign**

   A new Breakpoint named **Custom Tablet** is added between the Desktop and Tablet Portrait Breakpoints.

3. Rename a Breakpoint.

   ☐ click the words **Custom Tablet** and replace the text with **Larger Tablet**

   You can have up to five Breakpoints in Adobe Captivate. Using this feature, you can create layouts to meet the needs of the most common devices (and their unique sizes) used by your learners.

4. Delete a Breakpoint.

   ☐ with the **Larger Tablet** Breakpoint selected, click **Delete selected breakpoints**

   ☐ click the **Yes** button

5. Save and close the project.

Positioning Breakpoint Objects

When working with Responsive Projects, slide objects can move and resize dramatically depending upon the Breakpoint being viewed. Captivate allows you to anchor objects to the slide or to other objects.

Guided Activity 69: Position and Smart Position Objects

1. Open **MinMaxMe.cptx** from your Captivate2019BeyondData folder.

2. Open the Master Slide panel (**Window > Master Slide**).

3. Insert an object on the Main Master slide.

   ☐ ensure the **Main Master** is selected (the Main Master slide is the largest of the masters and has the word **Nimble** just beneath it)

   ☐ ensure the **Desktop** Breakpoint is selected

   ☐ choose **Media > Image**

   ☐ open the **Captivate2019BeyondData** folder

   ☐ from the **images_videos** folder, open **LogoCropped.bmp**

   The image is inserted in the middle of the Desktop view.

   ☐ on the **Position Inspector**, **Object Position [Absolute]** area, change the **Top** percent to **80**

   ☐ change the **Left** percent to **3**

   ☐ change the **Object Size Width** percent to **8%**

   ☐ if necessary, change the **Object Size** Height to **Auto**

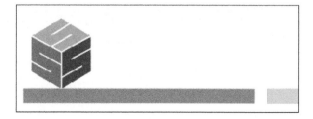

4. Review each of the project's Breakpoints.

   Notice that the image moves up a bit on each of the views. There will be instances where you're okay with an image moving higher on the view, but in this instance, you'd like the logo to stay in the same position, relative to the Breakpoint size.

5. Select the **Desktop** Breakpoint.

6. Zoom far enough away from the slide so that you can see the entire slide (and part of the surrounding Scrap Area).

7. Enable Smart Positioning.

   ☐ select the logo and, on the bottom of the **Position Inspector**, select **Smart Position** (if necessary)

8. Anchor an object to the bottom of the slide.

   ☐ ensure the logo is still selected

   ☐ at the top of the slide, drag the top **Smart Position marker** (it's the gray object just above the 80%) down to the **bottom** of the slide

   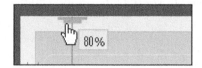

   ☐ when you see a horizontal line across the **entire bottom width of the slide**, release your mouse

   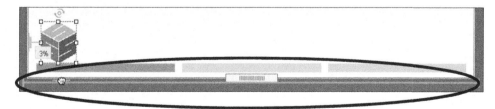

9. Review the Tablet and Mobile Breakpoints.

   The position of the logo is better—it does not float up as high on the slide as before. However, notice how small the logo gets, especially in the Mobile Portrait layout. Maybe your organization has standards for how big or small the logo can be. You'll set a maximum and minimum object size next.

---

10. Set the maximum and minimum size of an image.

❏ select the **Desktop** layout

❏ select the logo and, on the **Position Inspector**, expand the **Advanced** area

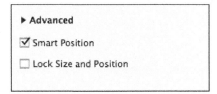

❏ change the **Min-Height** to **50** px and the **Min-Width** to **50** px

11. Review the Tablet Portrait and Mobile Portrait layouts.

   Notice that the size of the logo remains consistent from layout to layout. In fact, thanks to the Min-Height and Min-Width settings, the logo can never get smaller than 50 pixels.

12. Exit the Slide Master.

Responsive Object Styles

Do you have a need to use different fonts or font sizes for your text captions on each Breakpoint? Although you can manually change the font formatting on each caption, Breakpoint by Breakpoint, it would be much more efficient to use the Object Style Manager.

Guided Activity 70: Edit Breakpoint Object Styles

1. Ensure that the **MinMaxMe** project is still open.

2. Edit the styles used by the Breakpoints.

   ❑ choose **Edit > Object Style Manager**

   ❑ from the list at the left, expand **Standard Objects**

   ❑ expand **Smart Shapes**

   ❑ select **Title**

   ❑ from the **Text Format** area at the right, notice that there are settings for each of the three project Break Points.

3. Select each Break Point and change the text formatting as you see fit (perhaps a smaller font size for the Mobile Portrait layout than the other two layouts or a different font for the Tablet Portrait layout, it's up to you).

4. When finished, click the **OK** button and observe the text formatting changes you've applied to each Break Point.

5. Save and close the project.

Fluid Box Mode

I've mentioned a couple of times that there are two responsive development modes in Captivate: Fluid Boxes and Breakpoints. Between the two, Fluid Boxes are easier and faster to work with. You've spent a bit of time playing with a responsive project that was created using Breakpoint mode.

Fluid Box mode might be ideal if you're looking to create a basic layout fast and you're not overly concerned with exact page positioning of slide objects. You can create vertical or horizontal layouts with Fluid Boxes, and you can switch between them should you change your mind.

Once you add Fluid Boxes to a slide, the boxes behave much like tables and table cells. You click within a cell (a Fluid Box) and insert media, such as captions, images, and buttons. After you've added the media, you can control several aspects of the Fluid Boxes such as how the content flows when viewed on different devices, and add spacing between the Fluid Box contents.

If you've created projects using Captivate's standard development mode (meaning the slide layouts are not responsive), those non-responsive projects can be converted to responsive eLearning.

Guided Activity 71: Save a Standard Project As Responsive

1. Open **RespondMe** from the Captivate2019BeyondData folder.

   This is a standard project created using Captivate's typical development mode. It is not responsive.

2. Preview the project as **HTML5 in Browser**.

   The project plays just fine. However, if you resize the browser window, the content does not re-flow as the window size changes.

3. Close the browser.

   Because this is a standard project, responsive features are disabled. For instance, on the Toolbar, notice that the **Fluid Box** tool is not available.

4. Convert a standard project to a responsive layout.

☐ choose **File > Save As Responsive**

Because it's possible that there are objects in the project that won't work if the project becomes responsive (such as rollover captions and Flash animation), an alert appears.

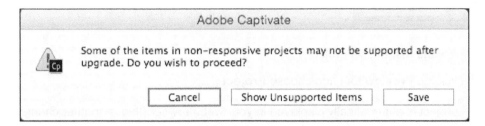

☐ click **Show Unsupported Items**

The HTML5 Tracker is empty indicating that this project will work fine as a responsive project.

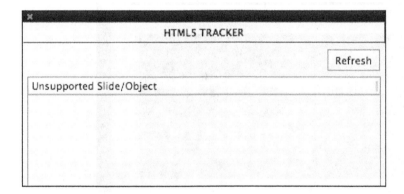

☐ close the HTML5 Tracker

☐ choose **File > Save As Responsive** again

☐ click the **Save** button

☐ change the name of the file to **RespondMe_Converted** and then save it to the Captivate2019BeyondData folder

Nothing dramatic appears to change in the project. However, in the upper left of the window is a **Layout Preview in** area. In addition, notice that the Fluid Box tool is now available.

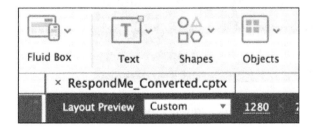

There's also a **Preview Slider** in the upper right of the window. You won't see any of these features in a standard Captivate project.

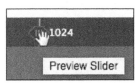

5. Preview the responsive project.

   ☐ click the **Preview** tool and choose **Project**

   The project is automatically displayed in your web browser (this is another change from a standard project where Previewing > Project displays the preview outside of the browser).

   ☐ drag the preview slider left and right

   Notice that the slide objects resize/re-flow as the screen size changes.

Your once standard, non-responsive project is suddenly responsive.

6. Close the browser.

7. Save and close the project.

Guided Activity 72: Insert and Name Fluid Boxes

1. Open **FluidBoxMe** from the Captivate2019BeyondData folder.

   This is a more generic version of the Our Management Team project than you've seen previously. It is already a responsive project. Slide 3 is a blank slide awaiting your input.

2. Add Fluid Boxes to a slide.

   ☐ go to slide **3**

   ☐ on the toolbar, click **Fluid Box**

   ☐ choose **Vertical > 3**

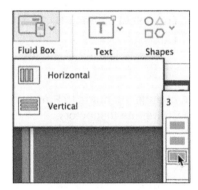

   Three Fluid Boxes are added to the slide—at least that's how it appears. In reality, there are four Fluid Boxes. There is a large one that you really cannot see (it's the parent Fluid Box), and it contains three equally sized child Fluid Boxes).

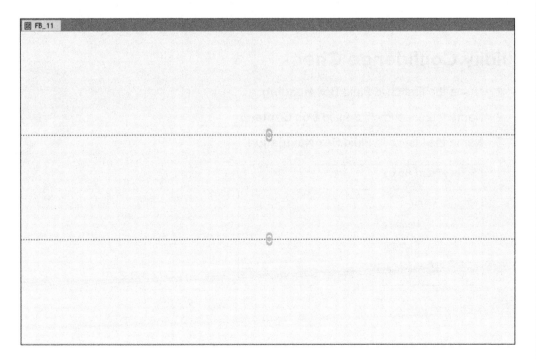

NOTES

3. Review the parent/child relationship of the Fluid Boxes.

   ❑ open the **Properties Inspector**

   ❑ from the **Select Fluid Box** area, notice there are four items

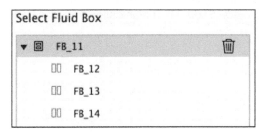

Each object represents the slide's four Fluid Boxes. The object named **FB_11** is the parent box; the remaining boxes are its children.

4. Name Fluid Boxes.

   ❑ with **FB_11** selected on the Properties Inspector, change the name to **Parent** (you can change the name in the name area at top of the Properties Inspector)

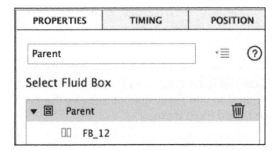

Fluidity Confidence Check

1. Name the first child Fluid Box **Heading**.

2. Name the second child Fluid Box **Content**.

3. Name the last child Fluid Box **Navigation**.

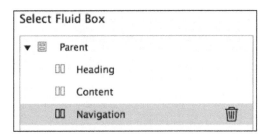

Guided Activity 73: Resize Fluid Boxes

1. Ensure that the **FluidBoxMe** project is still open.

2. Resize the child Fluid Boxes.

   ☐ with the **Parent** Fluid Box selected, drag the resizing handle for the first child box up until the box is approximately **1 inch tall**

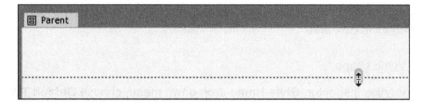

Note: Resizing the boxes might become an exercise in patience. Oftentimes for me, attempting to resize a Child box often deselects everything, and I have to go back to the Properties Inspector and select the Parent again. Should the Fluid Box Selector disappear on the Inspector, try clicking any corner of the Parent Fluid Box on the slide. Doing so typically allows you to select the Fluid Boxes on the Inspector. When you are attempting to resize, **the Parent must first be selected**, and you'll need to see a double-headed arrow as shown in the images above and below.

   ☐ with the **Parent** Fluid Box selected, drag the resizing handle for the last child box down until the box is approximately **1 inch tall**

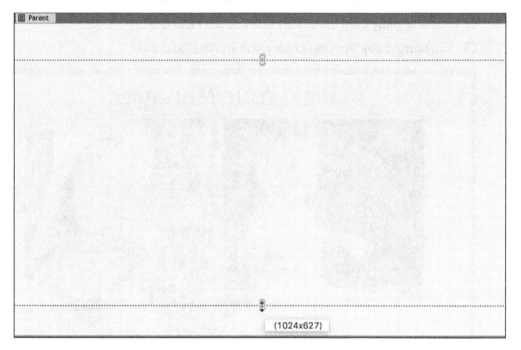

(1024x627)

NOTES

Guided Activity 74: Add Content to Fluid Boxes

1. Ensure that the **FluidBoxMe** project is still open.

2. Draw a Smart Shape in a Fluid Box.

   ☐ on slide **3**, click within the **Heading** Fluid Box

   ☐ on the toolbar, click **Shapes** and choose **Rectangle**

   ☐ draw a rectangle within the **Heading** Fluid Box that is approximately the same size as the Heading Fluid Box area

3. Apply a style to the shape.

   ☐ on the Properties Inspector, **Style Name** drop-down menu, choose **Default Title Smart Shape Style**

   ☐ double-click within the Shape and type **Pick Your Manager**

4. Use the Library to add images to a Fluid Box.

   ☐ select the **Content** Fluid Box (the middle, largest Fluid Box)

   ☐ from the upper right of the Captivate window, click **Library**

   ☐ drag **biff_baby** from the Library and into the Fluid Box

   ☐ drag **betty_baby** from the Library and into the Fluid Box

Content Confidence Check

1. Select the **Navigation** Fluid Box (the last Fluid Box).

2. Using the Shapes tool, draw a **Rounded Rectangle** in the box.

3. Type the following into the box: **Biff Bifferson**.

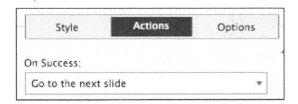

4. On the **Properties Inspector**, select **Use as Button**.

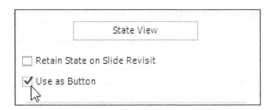

5. On the **Properties Inspector > Actions** tab, ensure **Go to the next slide** is selected for **On Success**.

6. On the **Properties Inspector > Others area**, select **Hand Cursor**.

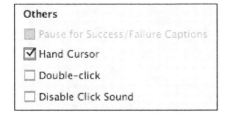

7. Duplicate the button and change the new button's text to **Betty Bifferson**.

NOTES

8. Change the **On Success** Action to **Jump to slide** and choose slide **5**.

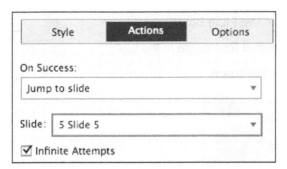

I think you'll agree that adding content to Fluid Boxes is pretty easy. But are you concerned at all with how close the objects are to each other? Fortunately, it's easy to add both horizontal and vertical space between objects.

9. Click to the **right** of the **Betty** image (to deselect the image and display the Fluid Box options on the Properties Inspector).

10. On the **Properties Inspector > Fluid Box Selector**, select the **Navigation** Fluid Box.

11. On the **Properties Inspector > Padding** area, change both the Horizontal and Vertical padding to **20** px.

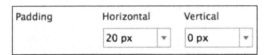

12. Change the **Padding** for the **Content** Fluid Box to 20 px.

13. Preview **From this Slide** and notice as you drag the window size slider, the content automatically re-flows to the new window size.

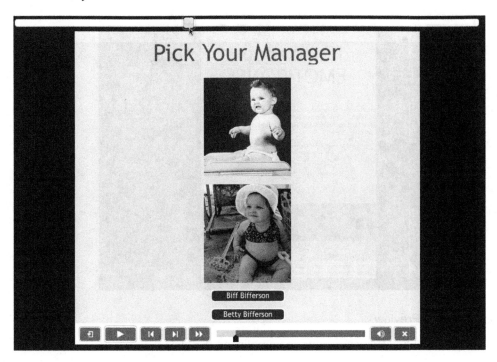

14. Close the browser and return to the Captivate project.

15. Save and close the project.

16. Open the **FluidWrapMe** project from the Captivate2019BeyondData folder.

    This project, created by fellow Captivate developer **Dr. Pooja Jaisingh**, will give you an excellent overview of how to control object Flow and Wrap.

17. Click in the **upper right corner** of the **Title** Fluid Box (to activate the Fluid Box options on the Properties Inspector).

18. On the Properties Inspector, use the **Fluid Box Selector** to select the **Parent** Fluid Box (it's called **FB_47** in this project).

19. From the **Content Flow** area, change the flow from **Vertical** to **Horizontal**.

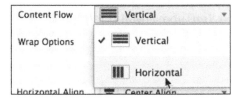

    The layout instantly changes from a top-to-bottom layout to a left-to-right layout.

20. From the **Content Flow** area, change the flow back to **Vertical**.

21. Preview the project.

22. As you resize the preview window (by dragging the slider), notice how the emoticons wrap to the next line, one by one.

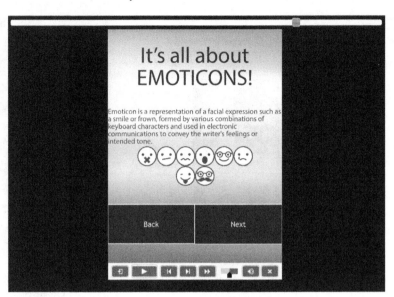

23. Close the Preview.

24. Select the Fluid Box containing the emoticons (FB_51).

25. Change the Wrap Options to **Symmetrical**.

26. To the right of Symmetrical, click **Layout Preview**.

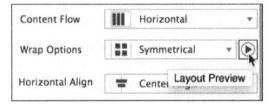

Thanks to the Symmetrical Wrap option, this time the emoticons wrap in equal groups.

27. Close the project (there is no need to save it).

Note: Looking to learn even more about Fluid Boxes? Check out fellow Captivate developer **Paul Wilson's** awesome video on YouTube: tinyurl.com/y4p5b8p7.

Module 10: Reporting Results

In This Module You Will Learn About:

And You Will Learn To:

LMS Reporting Options

Later in this module, you will publish a project and then upload it into a Learning Management System (LMS) called Inquisiq (you'll learn about Inquisiq on page 228). *But not so fast.* Before a project can be used with an LMS, you have to set up some reporting options and become familiar with the following: Sharable Content Object Reference Model (SCORM), Aviation Industry Computer-Based Training Committee (AICC), Sharable Content Object (SCO), and the Manifest File.

Sharable Content Object Reference Model

Developed by public- and private-sector organizations, SCORM is a series of standards that specifies ways to catalog, launch, and track course objects. Courses and management systems that follow the SCORM specifications allow for sharing of courses among federal agencies, colleges, and universities. Although SCORM is not the only standard, it is one of the most common. There are two primary versions of SCORM: version 1.2, released in 1999, and version 2004.

During the remaining activities in this module, you will prepare and then publish a project to a SCORM-compliant LMS.

Aviation Industry Computer-Based Training Committee

AICC is an international association that develops guidelines for the aviation industry in the development, delivery, and evaluation of training technologies. When you publish your Captivate projects, you can specify SCORM or AICC compliance, but not both. Not sure which one to pick? Talk to your LMS provider for information on which one to use. When in doubt, consider that AICC is older and more established than SCORM, but SCORM is the standard most often used today.

Tin Can API

Today's learners are consuming eLearning content using a vast array of devices (PCs, Macs, and mobile devices, such as the iPad). And learners are working outside of traditional LMSs. In spite of these challenges, educators still need to capture reliable data about the learner experience.

The problem with data collection is that you need an expensive LMS to store the data. And your learners need live access to the LMS so that they can send the data. As mentioned above, the most widely used LMS standard for capturing data is SCORM. SCORM allows educators to track such things as learner completion of a course, pass/fail rates, and the amount of time a learner takes to complete a lesson or course. But what if a trainer needs to get scores from learners who are collaborating with other students using social media? What if the learners don't have access to the Internet?

The new Tin Can API allows training professionals to gather detailed data about the learner experience as the learner moves through an eLearning course (either online or offline). According to the Tin Can API website, "Tin Can, the **Experience API**, captures data in a consistent format about a person or group's activities from many technologies. Very different systems are able to securely communicate by capturing and sharing this stream of activities using Tin Can's simple vocabulary."

If the Tin Can API is supported by your LMS, you'll be happy to learn that it's also fully supported in Adobe Captivate. All you need to do is choose **Quiz > Quiz Preferences**. From the Reporting group, select **Enable reporting for this project**, select an LMS, and then select **TinCan** as the Standard.

Sharable Content Objects

Sharable Content Objects (SCOs) are standardized, reusable learning objects. An LMS can launch and communicate with SCOs and can interpret instructions that tell the LMS which SCO to show a user and when to show it. Why should you know what a SCO is? Actually, your Captivate projects are SCOs once you enable reporting. Then you publish the project as a Content Package so that it can be uploaded into an LMS.

Guided Activity 75: Set Quiz Reporting Options

1. Open **LMS_Me** from the Captivate2019BeyondData folder.

2. Enable Reporting for the project.

   ☐ choose **Quiz > Quiz Preferences**

   The Preferences dialog box opens; Reporting is selected from the Quiz category.

   ☐ from the top of the dialog box, select **Enable reporting for this project**

   ☐ from the **LMS** drop-down menu, select **Other Standard LMSs**

   ☐ from the **Standard** drop-down menu, choose **SCORM 1.2**

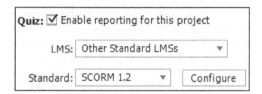

   SCORM 1.2, although an older standard, is still used by many LMS vendors today. Inquisiq (the LMS you will use shortly) supports SCORM 1.2, SCORM 2004, and AICC.

3. Set the Status Representation options.

   ☐ from the **Status Representation** area, select **Incomplete ---> Complete**

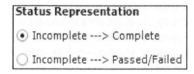

   This project isn't a conventional quiz—there are no question slides. Nevertheless, you can set interactive objects (such as buttons or click boxes) to report a value/score to the LMS, much like you can by assigning a point value to a question slide.

---

4. Set the Success/Completion Criteria.

❏ from the **Success/Completion Criteria** area, select **Slide views and/or quiz**

❏ deselect **Slide Views**

❏ select **Quiz** and ensure **Quiz is Passed** is selected from the drop-down menu

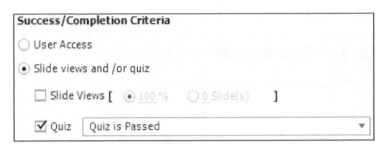

5. Set the Data to report.

❏ from the **Data To Report** area, select **Percentage**

Again, this project isn't a quiz. However, one of the objects in the lesson (a button) is going to be assigned a point value, making it a scoreable object. In essence, the lesson scores like a quiz, but does not contain any questions or answers. When the learner finishes with the lesson, the LMS displays the results as 100% Complete.

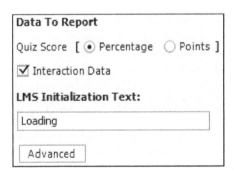

Note: The LMS Initialization Text field shown is not supported by every LMS. Fortunately, the LMS shown in this book supports the feature. Anything you type in the field appears just before the lesson begins to play for the learner. In essence, LMS Initialization Text serves as a second lesson Preloader. You can edit the text, if you'd like, or leave it set to the default (Loading).

Not every LMS fully supports the features in this dialog box (or the Manifest settings that you will set up next). And even if every feature is supported, each LMS could treat the features differently. One option might work perfectly in LMS A, while yielding totally different results in LMS B. The only consistent thing I have found when working with LMSs is that they can be inconsistent. Consult with your LMS provider to get an idea of what will work and what won't.

Manifest Files

The Manifest file allows your published Captivate projects to be used and launched from a SCORM 1.2- or 2004-compliant LMS. When you publish projects, you can have Captivate create the Manifest file for you. The Manifest file that Captivate creates contains XML tags that describe the organization and structure of the published project to the LMS.

Guided Activity 76: Create a Manifest File

1. Ensure that the **LMS_Me** project is still open (the Quiz Preferences dialog box should also still be open via **Quiz > Quiz Preferences**).

2. Show the Manifest file options.

   ❑ from the top of the dialog box, ensure **SCORM 1.2** is selected (from the **Standard** drop-down menu)

   ❑ click the **Configure** button

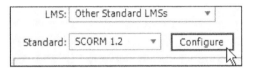

The Manifest dialog box opens.

3. Set up the course information.

   ❑ in the **Identifier** field, type **course_001**

The Identifier specifies a name used by the LMS to identify different manifests.

   ❑ in the **Title** field, type **File Management**

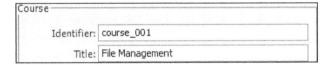

The Title is seen by learners as they access the course on the LMS. A Description is not required. Depending on the LMS you use, the text may or may not appear in the LMS. If the feature is not supported by the LMS, it will likely be ignored, just like the Title. You'll leave the Description blank for this lesson.

The Version number, which you left selected, can be used to distinguish manifests with the same identifier.

There are two other choices in the Course area: Duration and Keywords. Duration lets you show how long it takes to complete the Captivate project. Keywords allows you to specify a short description. When the course is displayed via a browser, such as Internet Explorer, the description and Keywords can be searched like any web page.

4. Set up the SCO information.

☐ in the **SCO Identifier** field, type **sco_001**

The Identifier, which cannot contain spaces, specifies a name used by the LMS to identify different SCOs.

☐ in the **Title** field, type **Creating New Folders**

The Title you just typed shows up in the LMS. Although you can use spaces in the Title name, you should consider using short descriptive phrases.

☐ click the **OK** button to close the Manifest dialog box

☐ click the **OK** button to close the Preferences dialog box

Nothing about your project changes physically. However, once the project is published, it will automatically be zipped and capable of communicating with any SCORM-compliant LMS.

Advanced Interaction

If you are uploading content into an LMS, you will find the Advanced Interaction dialog box one of Captivate's most useful features. Using this handy screen, you can quickly determine what any of the interactive elements (click boxes, question slides, buttons, text entry boxes, etc.) are doing for the whole project—in one central location. You can determine, with a quick glance, which elements in your project are scoring, the number of allowed user-interaction attempts, the value of each interaction, and if the interaction should be tracked by the LMS. Prior to the Advanced Interaction feature, Captivate developers had to suffer through the laborious process of opening each slide and reviewing the interactive settings, object by object. If the developer missed just one object, the score sent to the LMS would likely be incorrect—a problem not discovered until after the lesson was published, uploaded to the LMS, and tested.

Guided Activity 77: Report a Button Interaction

1. Ensure that the **LMS_Me** project is still open.

2. Enable Reporting for an object.

   ☐ go to slide **10**

   ☐ on the slide, double-click the large **Get Credit** button

   ☐ on the **Properties Inspector**, select the **Actions** tab

   ☐ from the **Reporting** area, select **Include in Quiz**

   ☐ change the Points to **100**

   ☐ select **Add to Total**

   ☐ select **Report Answers**

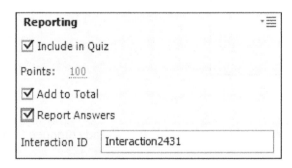

There is an Interaction ID area containing an ID. Although some management systems require an Interaction ID for every object reporting a score, others do not. When in doubt, leave the Interaction ID set to the default value.

Guided Activity 78: Adjust Slide Object Interaction

1. Ensure that the **LMS_Me** project is still open.

2. Display the Advanced Interaction window.

   ❑ choose **Project > Advanced Interaction**

   The Advanced Interaction window opens. Notice that the total score (as shown at the top of the dialog box) indicates that the lesson will report more than a perfect score to the LMS (112 points instead of 100). If you leave things the way they are, your LMS will likely report the results of the lesson incorrectly. Ideally, your lessons will never be worth more than 100 points.

   Total: 112 Points

3. Disable reporting for two slide objects.

   ❑ from the **Slide/Object** column, row **3**, click the words **Click Box**

   Captivate jumps to slide 3 and automatically selects the Click Box on the slide.

   ❑ from the **Reporting** area of the **Properties Inspector**, notice that the Click Box is being included in the Quiz and is reporting a score of 11 points.

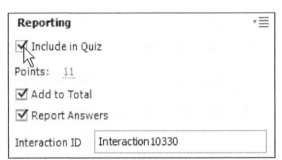

   ❑ deselect **Include in Quiz**

   On the Advanced Interaction window, the total point value has already dropped from 112 to 101.

   ❑ still working within the Advance Interaction window, row **6**, click the words **Click Box**
   ❑ from the **Reporting** area of the Properties Inspector, deselect **Include in Quiz**

   Notice that the total score for your lesson is now set to 100 points.

   Total: 100 Points

4. Close the Advanced Interaction window and then save your work.

SCORM Preview

You will soon publish your Captivate project as a SCORM-compliant package so that it can report scores and interactions to an LMS. However, there could be something in your project that isn't reporting correctly. You won't know there's a problem until after you publish the project, upload it to your LMS, and then test it. To save you a significant amount of work, Captivate allows you to verify that your lesson will report accurately with an LMS via a feature called Preview in SCORM Cloud. An LMS preview window appears allowing you to debug your project in preview mode and view SCORM communication logs.

Guided Activity 79: Preview in SCORM Cloud

1. Ensure that the **LMS_Me** project is still open.

2. Preview in SCORM Cloud.

   ☐ choose **Preview > Preview in SCORM Cloud**

   The SCORM Cloud dialog box opens.

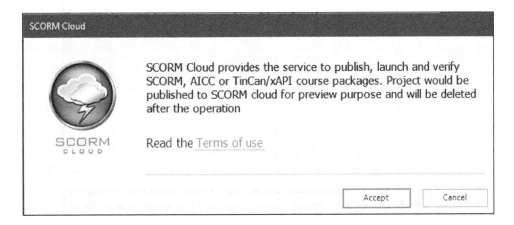

   ☐ click the **Accept** button

   The project is uploaded to the SCORM Cloud.

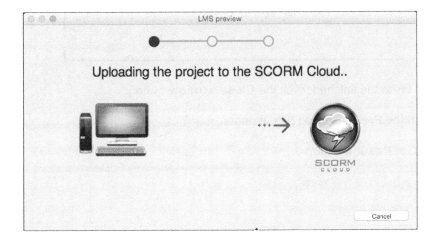

   The lesson opens in a preview window. You can work through the lesson just as if it was published to an LMS.

☐ click through the lesson as prompted onscreen

As you move through the lesson, errors will be reported in the Communication logs area at the bottom of the preview. (There shouldn't be any errors because your lesson is, of course, absolutely perfect!)

☐ when you get to the credit screen, click the **Get Credit** button

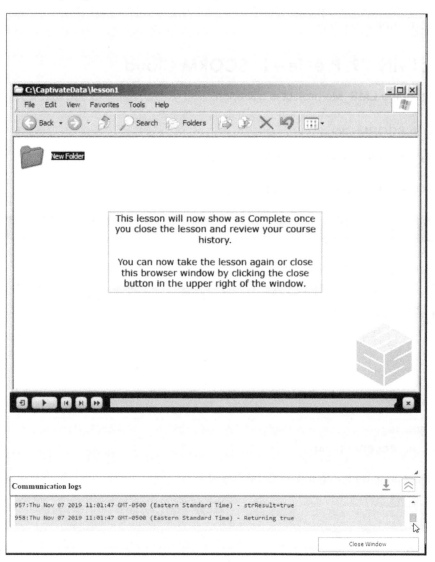

☐ when the lesson is finished, click the **Close window** button

The Relaunch the Preview dialog box appears.

☐ click the **Get Results** button

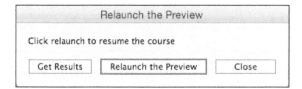

The Results window opens. At the bottom of the window, you can see that your lesson was worth 100 points, and it scored correctly. Based on these results, you shouldn't have any errors after uploading the lesson to a SCORM-compliant LMS.

3. Close the Results window.

4. Close the **Relaunch the Preview** dialog box.

Content Packages

When you selected **Enable reporting for this project** via **Quiz > Quiz Preferences** (see page 217), your Captivate project basically became a Sharable Content Object (see SCO, page 217). Now that the lesson is a SCO, you need to Publish the lesson as a zipped Content Package so that it can be uploaded into an LMS. Once the SCO is published as a zipped file, it comes a Content Package. The package contains your Captivate lesson, quiz settings, reporting data, the manifest file, and other support files.

Guided Activity 80: Publish a SCORM Content Package

1. Ensure that the **LMS_Me** project is still open.

2. Review the Quiz Pass/Fail settings.

   ☐ choose **Quiz > Quiz Preferences**

   ☐ from the **Quiz** category at the left, select **Pass or Fail**

   From the **Pass/Fail Options** area, notice that the options have been set to 100% or more of total points to pass.

Pass/Fail Options: ⊙	100	% or more of total points to pass

   Because you enabled Reporting for the button on slide 10 and set its value to 100 points, a learner who clicks the "Get Credit" button on slide 10 will pass the "Quiz."

   ☐ click the **Cancel** button

3. Publish a Content Package.

   ☐ choose **File > Publish**

   Notice that **HTML5/SWF** is selected from the **Publish as** drop-down menu and that the **Project Title** is **CreateNewFolder**.

4. Specify a Publish destination for the published package.

   ☐ click the **Browse** button (the yellow folder) and choose the **Captivate2019BeyondData** folder

   Notice that Zip Files is selected. The Zip Files option is what creates the Content Package as you publish the lesson. Keep in mind that your published lesson is not just one file. In fact, there are several files that need to work together for the lesson to play and for the LMS to track and score it properly. Without the ability to create the Content Package, you would have to upload the published pieces into the LMS individually.

Publish as:	HTML5 / SWF ▾
Project Title:	CreateNewFolder
Location:	/Users/iconlogic/Desktop/Captivate2019BeyondData
	☑ Zip Files

5. Specify an Output Format.

   ❏ from the **Output Format** Options area, select **HTML5** (deselect SWF if necessary)

   ❏ from the right of the dialog box, ensure that **Scalable HTML content** is selected

With Scalable HTML content enabled, the eLearning content will always resize to the size of the learner's screen.

   ❏ click the **Publish** button

   ❏ click the **OK** button when the alert dialog box appears telling you the Publish process is complete

When you look in the **Captivate2019BeyondData** folder, you see a **CreateNewFolder.zip** file. This is the file you will soon import into the LMS. During the upload process, the Zip file is extracted, and the contents of the package are uploaded and then installed in the LMS.

☐ Name
💻 CreateNewFolder.zip

6. Save and close the project.

Uploading eLearning Content to an LMS

An LMS handles issues related to providing access to the content, delivery of the content, and student performance tracking/reporting. In short, an LMS is the backbone of a web-based training system.

Inquisiq

Inquisiq is an easy-to-use LMS created by ICS Learning Group (ICS). ICS (**www.icslearninggroup.com**) is a leading provider of computer-based training solutions, including custom content development, LMS implementation, and instructional design. In addition, ICS specializes in corporate communications and multimedia development for touch-screen kiosks, interactive media, corporate websites, and online content management systems.

During the next few activities, you will be guided through the steps necessary to access Inquisiq, set up a user account, upload a content package, and create a Course and Curriculum. When you have completed this book, you will have up to 30 days to continue using Inquisiq free of charge. At the end of the evaluation period, you can purchase the LMS directly from ICS if you'd like to continue using its LMS.

Course Catalogs

A Course Catalog, also known as a Curriculum, is the plan you develop that details what your learners need to know when taking your courses, assets needed to implement the plan, and the context in which learning and teaching take place. The Curriculum sets the methods, structure, organization, balance, and presentation of the courses.

Courses

Each course you create serves as a building block of the Curriculum. Courses as they relate to learning are a series of lessons or steps that, when completed, fulfill the plan specified by the Curriculum. Each of the following could be considered a course: lectures, discussions, simulations, assignments, tests, and exams.

> **Note:** You will next set up a free account on Inquisiq and upload the SCO you published on page 226. You must have Internet access to complete the remaining activities in this module.

Guided Activity 81: Create an Inquisiq LMS Account

1. Create a user account in Inquisiq.

   ☐ using a web browser go to **https://www.inquisiq.com/free-trial-signup/**

   The 30 Day Free Trial page opens.

2. Specify an Account Name and Password.

   ☐ fill in the **Inquisiq LMS Portal Name** field with your **first and last name** (the name you enter here will become part of the domain name used for your account... you can use **any name** except the one shown below, but don't use spaces)

   PORTAL NAME/URL [*]

   Must be at least 3 and no more than 50 characters and may only contain letters (not case-sensitive), numbers or dashes (-).

   biffbifferson

   ☐ type **a password** into the **Password** field

   ☐ continue to fill in the required fields (Name, Company Name, and Email) and agree to the User Agreements

   ☐ click the **Create My Free Trial** button

   Once the trial account has been set up, a confirmation screen opens.

   ✓

   ## Your Inquisiq Trial Account is ready:

   https://biffbifferson.inquisiqr4.com/

   An email has been sent to [ksiegel@iconlogic.com] with more information. Please save it for future reference.

   Note that your administrator Username is **administrator**. Your password is **the password you specified earlier**.

   ☐ click the **URL** link to open the start page for the LMS trial

3. Login to the LMS.

❏ at the far right of the screen, click the **Login In** button

The Login dialog box opens.

❏ type your **Username** and **Password** into the two fields (remember, your username is **administrator**)

❏ click the **Login** button

By default, you are taken to the Inquisiq Administrator Menu.

4. Upload a SCORM Package.

❏ from the **Content** area at the bottom of the page, click **SCORM Packages**

The SCORM Packages screen opens. (Be patient... it could take a few minutes.)

❐ from the **SCORM Packages** area, click the **Upload SCORM Package** link

The Upload screen appears.

❐ click the **Choose File** button

❐ navigate to **Captivate2019BeyondData** folder

❐ open the **CreateNewFolder.zip** file you created on page 226

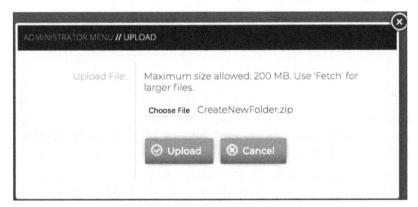

❐ click the **Upload** button

The package is imported into the LMS.

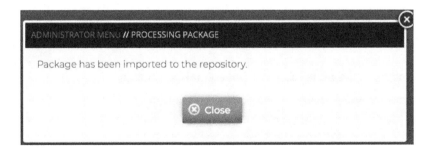

❐ click the **Close** button

Guided Activity 82: Create an LMS Course

1. Ensure that you are still logged into your Inquisiq account.

2. Create a new course.

   ☐ from the top of the window, click the **Administrator Menu** link

   ☐ from the **Content** area at the bottom of the page, click **Courses**

The Courses pages appears.

   ☐ from the **Courses** area, click **New Course**

   ☐ in the **Name** field, name the new course **File Management**

   ☐ in the **Short Description** field, type **These interactive lessons will teach you such fundamental Windows skills as creating folders, renaming folders, setting up a folder hierarchy, and Recycling.**

   ☐ from the bottom of the page, click the **Save Changes** button

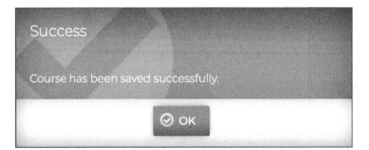

   ☐ click the **OK** button

Guided Activity 83: Attach a Lesson to a Course

1. Ensure that you are still logged into your Inquisiq account.

2. Attach a SCO to a course.

   ☐ from the top of the window, click the **Administrator Menu** link

   ☐ from the **Content** area at the bottom of the page, click **Courses**

The File Management course is listed among the courses within the LMS.

   ☐ click the **File Management** heading

The course opens for editing.

   ☐ click the **Lessons** tab

The **Lessons** page for the File Management course opens.

   ☐ click **New Lesson**

The Add Lesson window appears.

   ☐ in the **Name** field, name the lesson **Creating New Folders**

   ☐ in the **Short Description** field, type **This lesson will teach you how to create a new folder on your computer.**

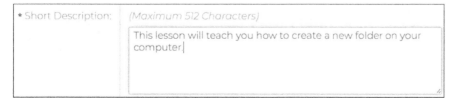

   ☐ from the **Type** area, click the **Select Package/Resource** button

Select Package/Resource

NOTES

The Packages window opens. This is where you find any content packages that you have uploaded to the LMS. In this instance, you see your CreateNewFolder.zip package that you uploaded earlier, along with several assets that are included with the Inquisiq trial account.

☐ select the **CreateNewFolder.zip** package

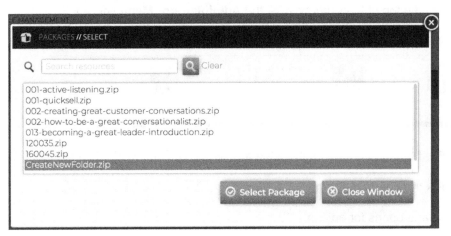

☐ click the **Select Package** button

☐ from the list of resources, select **sco_001_RES**

☐ click the **Select Resources** button

☐ click the **Save Changes**

☐ close the remaining open window

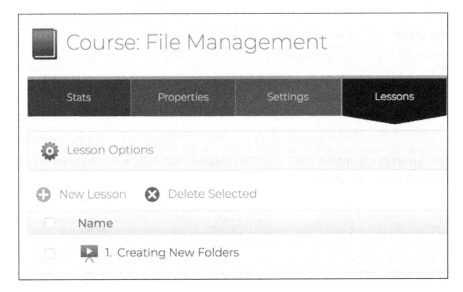

3. Publish a course.

    ☐ from the top of the window, click the **Administrator Menu** link

    ☐ from the bottom of the window, click **Courses**

    ☐ from the **Options** column, click the gray check mark for the **File Management** course

    Course is not Published - Click to Publish

    You will be asked to confirm the Publish action.

    Are you sure you want to publish this course?

    Cancel   OK

    ☐ click the **OK** button

    Once the course is published, the gray check mark turns green. The final steps are to create a Catalog and attach the File Management course to the catalog so that it can be accessed by your online learners.

Guided Activity 84: Create an LMS Catalog

1. Ensure that you are still logged into your Inquisiq account.

2. Add a Catalog (Curriculum) to the LMS.

   ❏ from the top of the window, click the **Administrator Menu** link

   ❏ from the bottom of the screen, click **Course Catalog**

   ❏ click **New Catalog**

The Add Catalog window appears.

   ❏ in the **Name** area, type **Windows Training**

   ❏ in the **Short Description** area, type **Everything you ever wanted to know about Windows, but were afraid to ask.**

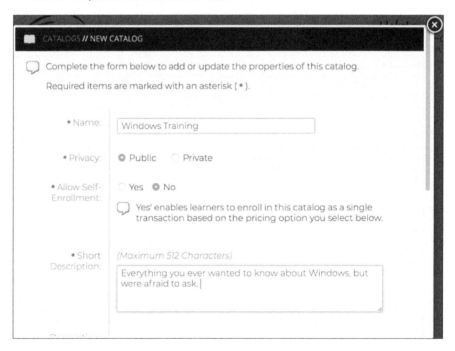

   ❏ from the bottom of the window, click the **Save Changes** button and close the window

The new catalog now appears in the Course Catalogs menu.

```
├─ Industrial Manufacturing - Sample Courses
├─ Windows Training
└─ File Management
```

Guided Activity 85: Attach a Course to a Catalog

1. Ensure that you are still logged into your Inquisiq account.

2. Attach a course to a catalog.

   ☐ select the **Windows Training** Catalog

   ☐ at the far right of the window, click **Add Course(s) To Catalog**

The Courses window opens. The File Management course you added is included within the list, along with other courses included in the Inquisiq trial account.

   ☐ select the **File Management** course

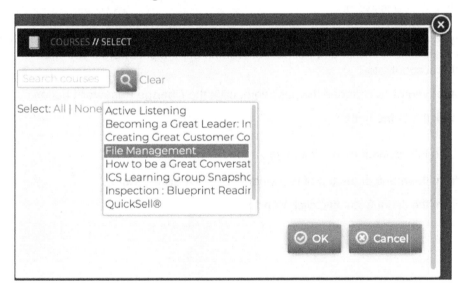

   ☐ click the **OK** button to close any open dialog boxes

Guided Activity 86: Test an eLearning Course

1. Logout of the LMS.

   ☐ at the upper right of the LMS window, click the **Log Out** link

   You cannot test the lesson while logged in as an administrator. The Inquisiq trial account includes a "learner" account that allows you to test the course.

2. Login to the LMS using the learner account.

   ☐ at the upper right of the LMS window, click Log In

   ☐ type **learner** into the **Username** field

   ☐ in the **Password** field, type **inquisiq**

   ☐ click the **Login** button

   Because this is the first time you are using the "learner" account, you are required to create a new password.

   ☐ type any password you like (you can use the same password that you used when you created the administrator account but remember the password if you want to access the account later)

   ☐ after you have changed the password, click the **Change Password** button

   ☐ click the **Done** button

3. Test the File Management course you added earlier.

   ☐ from the menu at the top of the window, click **Course Catalog**

   ☐ from the list of Catalogs, click **Windows Training**

   Catalog: Windows Training

   Courses: 1

   Everything you ever wanted to know about Windows, but were afraid to ask.

   The File Management course you created, published, and attached to the catalog is the only course available. In a real catalog, there would likely be multiple courses, each containing multiple lessons.

   ☐ click the **File Management** course title and then click the **Enroll Now** button

❏ from the top of the page, click **My Account**

The course is available in the list of available lessons.

❏ click the green **Go** icon

Notice that the status of the Creating New Folders lesson shows as **Not Attempted**.

❏ from the right side of the window, click the green **Go** icon

4. Work through the lesson (click the **Continue** button on the first slide and then move through the lesson as instructed onscreen).

5. When you get to the end of the lesson, click the **Get Credit** button. (Remember, this button is worth 100 points and lets the LMS know that the learner has completed the lesson.)

6. When you reach the end of the lesson, close the lesson window. (After the window closes, the LMS saves the data.)

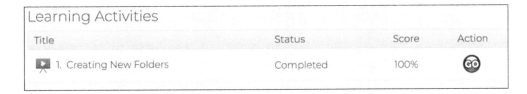

7. Click the word **here** to go back to the course details page.

And like magic, the status of the lesson has changed from **Not Attempted** to **Completed** and **100%**.

8. Logout of the LMS.

❏ click the **Log Out** link in the upper right of the window

9. Close the web browser.

Congratulations, you have completed this book! If you've also worked through *Adobe Captivate 2019: The Essentials (Second Edition)*, you have much of the knowledge you need to create compelling eLearning lessons. If you want to become a Captivate ninja,

practice will indeed make perfect. I encourage you to begin using Captivate right away... and use it frequently. There is truly no substitute for hands-on experience using the tool.

If you are looking for more information about Adobe Captivate, I encourage you to visit my blog (blog.iconlogic.com). I typically post articles a few times each week about Captivate and all things eLearning. You might also want to visit the Adobe's eLearning forum where you will find valuable tips and tricks on all things Captivate: https://elearning.adobe.com/.

Creating eLearning courses in Captivate has been fun for me. Yes, it's work, but it's enjoyable work. In time, I hope you come to love using Captivate as much as I do. And I hope your learners enjoy consuming your content even more.

Index

NOTES

NOTES

Notes

Made in the USA
Coppell, TX
27 August 2024

36527106R00144